T0114923

The Heresiad
Operatic Poetry

Song of Reason

The Heresiad
Operatic Poetry

Song of Reason

Ikeogu Oke

MANILA PUBLISHERS

MAKING
BOOKS
MATTER

First published in 2017 by
Kraft Books Limited
6A Polytechnic Road, Sango, Ibadan
Box 22084, University of Ibadan Post Office Ibadan
Oyo State, Nigeria
Telephone: +234 (0)803 348 2474, +234 (0)805 129 1191
Email: kraftbooks@yahoo.com
kraftbookslimited@gmail.com
Website: www.kraftbookslimited.com

This edition published in 2018 by
Manila Publishers Company
No. 3 Ambassador I. J. Udoyen Crescent
Opposite CBN Quarters, Karu New Layout
P. O. Box 10979, Area 10
Abuja 900001, FCT
Nigeria
Telephone: +234-(0)803-453-1501, +234-(0)705-556-4595
            +234-(0)808-234-8088, +234-(0)817-683-8484
Email: manilapublishers@gmail.com
Website: www.manilapublishers.com

ISBN 978-978-54688-4-7

Contents

For all who stand up for life,
For the harmony of thought and faith,
And for intellectual and creative liberty.

'I believe the time has come when some new warning has to be preached to us in the realm of politics. We all know that there was a time when a difference of religious belief was punished by physical punishment. Heretics were burned to death. Spiritual truth was believed to be almost material in character. But a sin which belongs to the realm of spirit can never be eradicated by punishment which is merely physical. The very idea that it could be is but an example of the beast in man speaking.'

– Rabindranath Tagore

'Keep no feeling of enmity for anyone.... Forgiveness is love at its highest power....Where there is forgiveness there is God Himself.'

– Guru Nānak

Preface
(Introducing Operatic Poetry)

'Written words can also sing.'

– Ngũgĩ wa Thiong'o,

'Sweet are the uses of adversity,
Which, like the toad, ugly and venomous,
Wears yet a precious jewel in his head;
And this our life, exempt from public haunt,
Finds … good in everything.'

– William Shakespeare

There is perhaps a yet-unexplored idea of poetry as an art form that transcends verse and goes on to embrace song, music and drama, resulting in what may be called *operatic poetry*. *The Heresiad* offers what may be a generally acceptable demonstration of the possibilities inherent in this type of poetry of which it hopes to be seen as an exemplification and to successfully inaugurate. To this end, it is essentially conceived and composed as a poem, as opposed to a libretto, though it can serve as the latter, or be modified to serve as such, for purposes of operatic performance. The story is primed for enactment and therefore dramatic.

The Heresiad has a utilitarian goal: to make a case for unhindered intellectual and creative freedom, what Nadine Gordimer sums up as 'freedom of the WORD', and for mutual respect and harmony between faith and thought, otherwise religion and intellectualism. In the light of this, intellectual and creative freedom is symbolised by Zumba, an author condemned to death for writing a book, religion by a monarch who condemns the author, and intellectualism by Reason who defends the author and so earns recognition for himself as the hero of the poem, hence its subtitle of Song of Reason.

Incidentally, Heresiad is coined from heresy, as Iliad, Aeneid and Dunciad might have been coined from Ilium, Aeneas and Dunces by Homer, Virgil and Alexander Pope respectively. And heresy is the alleged offence for which the monarch, who doubles as a powerful religious figure, condemns the author.

It is in recognition of the possibility of such a condemnation occurring in real life, as an untoward event without which the poem might not have been conceived, let alone written, that the above Shakespearean lines are evoked – as an epigraph – to allude to the poem as a manifestation of the sweet 'uses of adversity' and the penchant of art for finding 'good in everything'. The poem is an imaginative intercessory response to any such condemnation.

Regarding form, its lines are lyrical pentameters as opposed to the more conventional rhythmic pentameters. (Incidentally, lyrical pentameters are pentameters characterised by lyricism and adaptable to singing, while rhythmic pentameters are pentameters characterised by rhythm and adaptable to instrumental music.) Also, it is so literally a song that each of its lines is singable (an additional reason for the subtitle), unlike similar works whose authors have directly or obliquely identified as songs, such as Turold's *Chanson de Roland* (*The Song of Roland*), Vyāsa's *Bhagavad-Gītā* (the 'Lord's Song'), and Okot p'Bitek's *Song of Lawino*, but which they apparently did not expect to be rendered as songs – in addition to their being read (or performed) as poems. It is not only a literal song; each of its lines can also be set to music, as shown by the accompanying music scores. Its being a literal song validates Ngũgĩ wa Thiong'o's assertion that "written words can also sing," invoked as the first epigraph above.

The music scores – derived from various segments of its four cantos and entitled 'The Roaring Rage', 'The Forlorn Supplication', 'The Bold Resolution', and 'The Great Submission'[1] – are improvisational sample compositions meant to underscore its intrinsic musicality. Except for intermittent injections of authorial comments and narration, the entire story runs rather like a relay of declamations by two groups of disembodied but nominal voices. One of the groups comprises and is associated with the monarch, while the other includes and is connected to Reason.

As hinted above, the idea that inspired *The Heresiad* – essentially an anti-censorship poem that is also pro intellectualism and creative freedom, pro freedom of worship and the concomitant freedom to refrain from worship, and pro peace – makes it a veritable child of adversity: the author as the object of a death threat comparable to what obtained during the Inquisition, complete with the charge of heresy and whatnot. And as we know, actual incidents of such a threat, in their sometimes less vehement but no less disturbing modern-day manifestations in the various forms censorship can assume,

---

[1] 'The Great Submission' is derived from Canto IV, lines 455-472, 'The Roaring Rage' and 'The Forlorn Supplication' from Canto I lines 13-32 and 247-276 respectively, and 'The Bold Resolution' from Canto III, lines 607-620.

have impacted the lives and careers of many writers and poets, including Charles Baudelaire, Gustave Flaubert, James Joyce, D. H. Lawrence, Boris Pasternak, Alexander Solzhenitsyn, Nadine Gordimer, Chinua Achebe, Wole Soyinka, Ngũgĩ wa Thiong'o, Joseph Brodsky, Salman Rushdie, Orhan Pamuk, etc. It can therefore be regarded as a malaise spreading down the ages.

The transcendental powers of art derive partly from its capacity to turn such a threat and the attendant adversity to account, utilising its grossness to create a thing of lasting, if imperishable, beauty through its unique form of alchemy.

Ikeogu Oke
October 2016

The Voices

Zumba, an author

A monarch

Doom
Avenger
Sword
Machete
Axe
The monarch's page

⎱ The Faithfuls (the monarch's subjects)

Reason

Stone
Panther
Care
Bluff
Smithy
Reason's page

⎱ The Stalwarts (Reason's subjects)

Canto I

*A monarch, of a subterranean
kingdom, angered by some of the
contents of a book, pronounces a
death sentence on its author,
accusing him of heresy;
whereupon five of his subjects, the
Faithfuls, acting on his orders,
leave their kingdom for the earth
in search of the author, who
promptly goes into hiding, from
where he sends pleas to the
monarch to exercise restraint and
to Reason to intervene on his
behalf, and other related
occurrences.*

You tend the bloom of peace, The Heresiad,
Floral tokens from a Muse unheard,
For all in whom the East has met the West
That thought[2] and faith[3] may live without unrest,
And for all who stand up for life,
And up against the scourge of mortal strife.

                    *   *   *

You whose guidance I adjudge supreme,

---

[2] Thought: intellectualism.
[3] Faith: religion.

Bring aid to my peace-engendering scheme:
To explore a moral posture deemed perverse,
And resolve a conflict in the bounds of verse.   10

        *   *   *

I shall sing of how, eschewing strife,
Gracious Reason saved an author's life.

        *   *   *

And a monarch stirred up a row against a scorn
As he flared and blew his loud, belligerent horn:
'Ah! That's a mortal stepping on my toes,
Whose pride impels to take sides with my foes.'
And he charged his Faithfuls with a stern dispatch:
'Go! Turn all the kingdoms patch by patch.
Dig him out and fling him down to hell
While still dripping with my acid spell: 20
It's not our custom yet to spare a man
Who dares to glean our faults as best he can.
Such – a man of learning? Strike him dead!
And bring before my throne his upright head!
Ignore his soul or what may prove its luck:
Rather lose a lamb than forgo all the flock;
For such a man, if left to thrive on earth,
May void our honour and enforce our death.
Yes, death's the proper fate that awaits him.
I charge you now to move and quench his dream.   30
Ungracious though I know this is, let Zumba die!
I've marked a valley where his corpse will lie.'

*   *   *

Thus with lightning in his eyes, thunder in his voice,
The king dispatched his Faithfuls, yes, his boys.

*   *   *

Speaking thus, for all who cared to hear,
The ears of men began to twitch in fear;
And the monarch, having sensed their dread,
Made his visage glow more red and red.

*   *   *

At once, the Faithfuls, numbering five, with arms,
Left their kingdom, wearing sundry charms;   40
Up – towards our realm[4] – and up they marched:
The sky was stormy and the earth was parched!

*   *   *

Said Doom: 'We shall drag him down alive,
But not before I've cut him up in five:
The apostate that runs our master down,
And (with slander) strives to smear his crown.
He has flung all caution to the dogs
And must die rewarded by the logs
That burn with fury and a ceaseless fire,
There, beside our king's infernal mire.'   50
And he paused and thumped his hairy chest,
And let his voice collapse, as if depressed;

---

[4] Our realm (likewise in I. 284 and 'a realm' in I. 286): the earth.

And looking up a slope, along their way,
Doom, the Faithful, went ahead to say:
'This same man escaped our wrath before;
Yet he taunts us with his newfound lore.
What a strange event it'll be indeed
If his head survives his new misdeed.
Yes, we're meant to get him by and by,
Though his spirit may ascend the sky   60

To that illusory realm of pulchritude
For those who strove on earth for rectitude.
Down with that his pride, his heresy!
With that his learning, his apostasy!
Down with that his famed temerity
That impugns our faith's authority!'
      And Doom, the Faithful, licked and smacked his lips,
And then his speech was pregnant for its tips:
'A fly in the lair of a hungry spider:
What can save it? Not fate. Not strife either.'   70

                    *   *   *

      And brash Avenger promptly took the cue:
'How glad I'll be to watch his pieces stew –
A sumptuous dinner for some monster's table:
Clad with quilt and carved from snow-white marble.'
And he paused, and coughed, and shook his head;
And lumbering, yes, and bilious, went ahead:
'He's good for monsters' meat who must incur
The wrath of all of us with pride, and more.'
And now – as if his breath-supply was low,
But mindful not to let his distress show –   80

Avenger paused, and raised his iron spear,
And pulled across his face a veil of cheer;
Then his blotched, ironic tongue pursued:
'Mischance incurred for truth need not be rued.
And so I beg to keep his life, and well,
The rest of which is better spent in hell:
Where there's excess flame to ignite his ire,
And surplus brands to light his pen's desire,
And still support we drag him down alive[5]
In mangled pieces less than all but five   90
And stew him in a cauldron for the lord
That rules perdition with an iron sword;
For I'm sad, so sad, to think he's bound to die,
Who will let no glum Cerberus[6] lie.'

                    *   *   *

    And grim Sword, with his razor tongue, declared:
'A martyr's death is just a life deferred;
And truly you can't hack a saint[7] to death
While he's filled with God's eternal breath.
Raise your axe of threat; and off he flies,
To find a haven in the houseless skies.   100
Yet, must we now deny our blighted past
And watch him spite us in a mortal cast?
The word is *hurry* when the goal is *kill*
A man whose ways contemn our monarch's will.
Recall our history, then his pompous scorn,

---

[5] Compare with I. 43.
[6] Cerberus: the dog that guards the entrance to the underworld in classical mythology. The line hints at the idiom about letting sleeping dogs lie.
[7] A saint: a sarcastic allusion to the author.

And tear off *mercy* from your lexicon.
It's not my wish to let him stay alive,
Though cut in many thousands or in five.
There's a special trap to fetch his soul,
For seize him soul and body is our goal.   110
So now, brave comrades, marching by my side,
Let's go defend our future and our pride.
We must show the sky-bound sojourner:
The lord we serve is not a pardoner.'[8]

*   *   *

    And Machete was the next to speak,
His temper on a Himalayan peak:
'How his hubris rankles me indeed!
And his shrilling noise against our creed!'
And, leaning back, he drew a wheezing breath,
And, speaking, jabbed his fist towards the earth: 120
'But those for heaven[9] there are ways they live;
They neither care to see and yet believe,
Nor do they heed to reason, nor to proof,
That the cloud is no uncommon roof –
Where a pensive sovereign rests his feet
While enthroned on heaven's royal seat.
To them, earth is all devoid of love,
And all that's good is stationed up above:
Where rewards for their righteousness on earth,
And their piety even unto death,   130
God, they say, has done well to withhold
(To withhold, and make them manifold)

---

[8] Pardoner: someone who forgives.
[9] Those for heaven: a sarcastic classification meant to embrace the author.

Till when their austere piety shall be crowned
With joys whose depths are deeper than profound.
Their faith is certain. What about their hope?
Those who see but shut their eyes to grope!'
And he paused, and smiled, and what a quip,
Rendered with a pouted lower lip:
'And yet I'm happy that they've toed a way
That'll prove their folly on the Judgment Day.'   140

                    *   *   *

    And Axe, the zealot, was the next to speak.
His cool was thawing from a frozen peak
Whence, by distinct piece and rounded piece,
His words came dropping from the precipice;
And eager, as he was, to hide his fears,
He began straightaway to scold his peers:
'Why rave and argue all for nothing's sake?
We babble, boast, and court a grave mistake.'
Then he took a deep breath and began
To give the needed focus to their plan: 150
'Now let's set our drifting mission straight;
What we want is not the sinner's wraith;
Not his flesh to feed the king of hell.
In hell, ten inmates cram each dingy cell;
So bring a live man isn't why we're abroad;
Live men already swarm the netherworld.'
And speaking thus, and speaking all alone,
He added in a clear, unflinching tone:
'But this man must leave our faith at ease,
And not corrupt it with his mind's disease!'   160
Thus, he said, with sure finality,

And a tone that chimed with certainty.

       *   *   *

And souls in hell and heaven held their breath
As, day by day, the five approached the *earth*.
And soon Zumba was to know his stand:
A lonely pebble on an ocean's strand.
With roses men will stand with you, as one,
But court the prickles and you'll stand alone;
You'll stand alone, alone in all your pain,
Alone to know that men are inhumane.   170
So guard yourself from gullibility:
True friends are beacons of fidelity,
They'll shine for you in days of sweet delight,
And in days of gloom intensify their light.

       *   *   *

And our author, Zumba, found himself
Dogged by fears of dying by some elf;
And though he'd wish for heaven (in the sky?)
But – face the grim fact – should he wish to die?
And half by chance and half, it seemed, by choice,
He bowed his head and primed his bristly voice;   180
And, by evening, on that breezy day,
Our anguished author, Zumba, tried to pray.
No, to adapt the very words of his,
He sought to give his panic due release:
'I've pitched my tent with folly once again:
The sheep that beards the lion in his den;
And who, in this situation – though unwise –

Won't share my crippling fits of cowardice?
I will arise, before my hope is spent,
And go to beg the monarch to relent.   190
This mortal cast, though blemished, that I have,
I'll rather keep than hasten to the grave.
The earth (I've known of late) is cold to me.
How colder may a tomb of marble be?
Or of mud, for all its loneliness?
Or a granite sarcophagus nonetheless?'

              *   *   *

    The contours of his worries thus surveyed,
Our author, Zumba, bent his knees and prayed:
'Gracious monarch, please don't take my life.
Spare a thought for Mercy – that's my wife –   200
And our children who, without a crime,
May lose their father long before their prime.
I mean to right my wrong from word to word
And keep your favour as my king and lord.
Recall your agents, however far they've gone.
Please, forgive and watch my faith return.'
Here, our author would observe a pause,
And go ahead to speak, and plead his cause:
'Yes, to save our pride remains our right;
But then I think I feel a genuine fright: 210
To think I have to die for what I write,
The way a candle dies for yielding light.'

              *   *   *

    And so our author, having done with pleas,

Felt, as he'd say, 'some sense of ease.'
And risen from his knees, then to his feet,
He'd mutter, gazing at a lonely street:
'Those trees that can bend in a storm are the hardest to break,
And so I must bend and not break for my writing's sake.'

        *   *   *

   Yes, the monarch heard the forlorn pleas
That our author rendered on his knees.   220
And seeing 'the tables turned', he'd beam with smiles,
And shoot a joyous glance across the miles;
And then he'd raise a goblet 'for a toast',
And gulp the drink in it, and then would boast:
'Three hearty cheers for such diplomacy
That goes to prove my mind's efficacy,
For it lies beyond my strength to harm the man,
And so to take his life is not my plan.
Yet my threat has turned him to a mole:
Hushed, frightened, tucked inside a hole.'   230
And the monarch paused; he sneezed as well;
And resumed speaking (as he sipped prunelle):
'And though he'd let his temper rise and flare,
A king like me cannot be unaware
That it's vain for falsehood to contend
With truth that's ever destined to transcend.'
And he paused again, and went ahead,
Speaking (as he shook his tipsy head):
'But then I have a reason to rejoice
And mock his wisdom with my foolish voice: 240
I've put my simple mind to work, as fit,
And won a rare advantage to acquit.'

And he'd try to shout for joy but scream;
For, yes, the drink had taken charge of him.
It would leave him on the edge of sleep,
At ease and restful, in a drowsy heap!

*   *   *

And now our author, feeling quite subdued,
Addressed another plea from solitude,
A plea to Reason whom he'd fondly call
'My chosen lord and master, over all.'   250
He'd choose a lightless cave where every sound
Would echo back in swift and full rebound.
And this was what our author, Zumba, said
With a mournful slant of tone and head;
This was what his worries gave a voice,
While alone, confined, immured from noise:
'My thoughtful master, shield and guardian light,
Please direct your attention to my plight:
I'm almost doomed for having used the pen
You named your beacon for my fellow men.   260
Come down quickly lest I come to rue
That I chose to pitch my tent with you,
As I've largely rued my faith in men,
Whose ways with me, for now, suggest disdain.'
And our author (rather tongue-in-cheek)
Observed a pause, and then resumed to speak:
'Yet, in my distress, I have come to know
A thing or two for which my tact may grow;
That one man's pain is another man's glory,
And one man's grief another's sweet story.'   270
And our author, Zumba, paused again,

And went ahead to plead, and plead with pain:
'Please secure my faltering human trust,
And save the iron of my faith from rust.
Move to void the price placed on my head;
Save your friend from this unnerving dread.'
Those – the words he addressed to Reason's ears;
And Reason listens to his friends; he hears.
Even to his foes he's all devotion,
For the neutral way he pays attention.   280

        *   *   *

   Now, along some sloping rocky grounds,
Fresh effusions made their vocal rounds
Among the members of the monarch's crew,
Our realm[10], their target, still beyond their view.
And now I make to reveal what they said
As they climbed towards a realm in dread.

        *   *   *

   You, who guide my vision, steer my tale,
Lead me on to labour and prevail;
You whose kind desire nudged my heart
To give a lifebuoy to a drowning art.[11]   290

        *   *   *

   Doom became the first to speak again,
His voice like thunder growling in the rain;

---

[10] Our realm: see footnote number 3.
[11] A drowning art: poetry.

Hear him, as his dam of fury burst:
'Only blood can slake a bloodhound's thirst!'
Then he raised his head above the rest,
And made a broad hood of his hairy chest;
Yes (his head above the brotherhood[12])
He made his chest mimic a cobra's hood;
Then, with hisses spreading from his tongue,
The wild tide of his fury rolled along: 300
'You wonder why my fury so distends?
Better foes forever than foes after friends.
Here's a fellow who had shared our dream
And drunk our tipple from the very brim;
Now he aims his darts to win our shame
And throws indeed to score the vicious aim.
Now he aims his arrows at our pride,
And shoots to pierce our joy on every side.
How, beyond our reach, his sole desire
Is drag our honour through his heathen's mire!   310
How he chews our rare faults like the cud
And throws them up with nausea – right on mud!
And then our secrets, locked up in his mind,
Are now unsafe, and shouldn't be left behind.
They need recovery through the very act
That'll bring him to his end for lacking tact;
And then the bloated pride of all his type
Will fall, deflated, for that sort of gripe
With which the Greeks, their cudgels hard as steel,
Flattened Troy and all her pompous will.'   320
And Doom, the Faithful, would observe a pause,
Whereupon his speech proceeded thus:
'And let me lead the way for all of us,

---

[12] The brotherhood: alludes to the Faithfuls (as a group).

And lead it to his ruin without remorse.
And so I say – before I hold my breath –
To "leave our faith at ease" is leave in death.'[13]
And silence drew a leash across his lips,
As he fiddled with his trifid whips.

*   *   *

And Avenger was the next to speak
(His voice was choppy; it was strangely weak):   330
'Yes, his[14] treachery almost stopped my breath;
Hence I've pledged to comb the whole of earth
Till his quisling's errant soul is found
And all its hubris driven underground.'
And he paused and, blinking, rubbed his eyes,
And pulled their lashes, with a string of sighs;
Then (his voice now weaker for its reach)
Our worthy Faithful would resume his speech:
'But why have itchy eyes – to prick my mind,
And leave my sense of duty undefined?   340
Or a sign that we won't blood our spears –
This sight immersed in orbits dripping tears?
And what's the import that my deep resolve
Is mixed with conflicts of the soul to solve?
Could it mean his blame is mine to share?
Could it mean my zeal should tread with care?
Does it urge against unchecked disgust
That a man, as said, betrayed our trust?

---

[13] Compare with I. 159.
[14] His: refers to the author, the tenor of whose 'heretical' writings the speaker considers a manifestation of 'treachery' towards him and other believers with whom the author once identified.

And against our drive to end his life,
And heap woe on his children and his wife?'   350

                    *   *   *

   Sword became the very next to speak,
And his tone was nimble, truly quick.
And these – I recall – were the things he said,
As he wagged his fist and shook his head:
'To me his treachery needn't quite amaze,
Having read the inscription at our base:
"Life's worst deceits are hatched in amity;
Trust cheap and rue your gullibility;
Ever deadly, never eaten; ever shy, never bitten;
Never trust, and be by no one smitten."   360
And we've also read – or heard it read –
That graffiti scrawled in chalky red,
And mossy green, across the western wall,
Where Avenger owned a wooden stall:
"If you trust be wary, as a must;
The way of treachery is the way of trust."
And don't we know the much they stand to lose,
Who dare to show disdain for those our views?
Or dare recall the ruin of Burkinabe,[15]
That treachery of the meanest sort, I say,   370
As trusting Thomas[16] trusted to his end,
And lost his life and sceptre to a "friend".
Now, some grave retains his sad remains.
A loser, yes, for all his trust and pains!

---

[15] Burkinabe: the people of Burkina Faso.
[16] Trusting Thomas: Capt. Thomas Sankara (1953-1987), the Head of State of Burkina Faso, killed in a palace coup.

Even the wicked – I recall in fact –
Shuddered at that mean, perfidious act.'
Sword observed a pause; he'd then proceed,
Go ahead to speak his mind – indeed:
'True, the author's blame is ours to share,
That we may better learn to trust with care;   380
But face the fact that, with the harm he's done,
Our quest towards redress is well begun:
A full redress that'll surely bring to naught
The fame and glory that he seems to court.'
Here, his racy tongue would come to rest,
With acid fury burning in his chest.

*   *   *

And Machete, having cleared his throat,
Started speaking on a cautious note:
'I think the mood is grossly overcast,
In which we rue the error of our past.'   390
And Machete sneezed, observed a pause,
And went on speaking with a hint of force:
'We'll be doomed to mockery as a whole
Should we not realise our present goal.
So let the errors of our past be gone,
Or pass from ruing them to endless scorn.
Who, of you, can see the taunts ahead,
Taunts whose flood can drown our monarch's head,
And yet be lenient while some mortal draws
Our honour nearer death's eternal jaws?   400
To me, the very fruit of leniency
Has rotted on the tree of clemency,
And this mind that has so veered

Into our secrets must be severed,
Severed from the frame that harbours it,
From its body – and its crass conceit.'
And he paused again, and went ahead,
Speaking, as his knuckles rubbed his head:
'And how I wish the task were mine alone,
For how the goad of vengeance spurs me on: 410
And why presume a man can find reprieve
Whose pardon is your king's prerogative?'

                    *   *   *

    And Axe (after Machete) spoke next;
His voice was urgent and his tone was vexed:
'Let's not dwell on that erroneous past!
We must deem it passed, and yes it's passed!
But let's rely on what our clerics say,
And learn to keep our nagging doubts at bay.
"The man," they say, "has once again blasphemed."
And must we bear "our Holy Writ defamed"?   420
Who "profanes our faith" is bound to die;
And who can boast the guts to question why,
Or wag a cynic's tongue to sow the seed,
The seed of doubt, in something long decreed.
I'll rather search for where to whet my blade
Than, being doubtful, miss the prize[17] ahead;
And then proceed to spend my time at drill,
Drenched in sweat, to improve my axing skill:
Success is our lot – once confident
That our tools and skills are efficient;   430

---

[17] The prize: an allusion to the author as a symbol of the reward expected for
his assassination.

But the wary, who must fret and quail,
Are ever well rewarded when they fail.
On those our clerics let us, yes, rely;
They say "his pompous soul deserves to die
Who, to appease his new academy,
Drags our mores in mud and infamy".
So, shall we proceed to clear his guilt
To that foundation on which it is built,
Clear it fully and inscribe his name
In our twice-eternal book of shame?   440
Shall we clear it? Clear it? Take his life?
And heap grief on his children and his wife?'[18]
This – the much he had to say, and said,
As his callused knuckles rubbed his head.

*   *   *

And then a rather curious voice emerged,
Emerged from the Faithfuls' ranks and charged,
And charged them (as it were) of prejudice,
Though by very subtle hints as these
(It was Machete's, and his tone was firm;
And this was his rejoinder – I affirm):   450
'To captious clerics do not play the fool,
For no mind but your own can fix the rule;
I mean each rule by which a book is judged.
A book needs studying before it is smudged;
Or rather, yes, before its author's hand
Is lopped off, as it were, in reprimand.
It's by works read, not presumed a blight,
That critics' views are proven wrong or right.

---

[18] Compare with I. 350.

And thus must our clerics all be judged
Through the book we have so far prejudged,   460
For which we're now inclined to quench the man,
Though we're yet to read it, while we can.
I'm part of this misnomer, I confess,
And so are all you Faithfuls, nonetheless.
Or who among us Faithfuls can have read
The book for which we seek the author's head?'
And Machete paused, and went ahead,
Speaking calmly, as he shook his head:
'I sense some wrong in how we march with hate
To drown each human censure of our faith;   470
But move I must, and move with much unease,
And wish we knew our faith was built[19] on peace.
And tell me: from a grim quest such as this,
Can more peace accrue than hate and crisis?'
Thus, and calmly, he would ask the rest,
Amid the startling doubts his words expressed.

*   *   *

Fresh from slumber, and with bated breath,
The monarch stretched a look towards the earth –
Where his Faithfuls, inching out of sight,
Seemed to climb towards the morning light,   480
Seemed to climb a skyward sandy slope,
With such ease as laid within their scope.
And his royal heart was more than glad,
So glad he turned and beckoned on a lad,
A sprightly page, a courier for his throne;
And pointing upwards, with a lucid tone,

---

[19] Built (likewise in II. 537): founded.

He addressed the lad, now waiting, yet untried:
'There – observe – a blurred sight – to my side –
Those Faithfuls climbing to the morning light.
They left from here to set his wrong aright   490
"Who," to quote some clerics for your lord,
"Has blasphemed against our glorious Word[20]".
But how he dreads our sword of nemesis,
And craves our pardon for his heresies,
His heresies which, with his blasphemies,
Make him the worst of our enemies;
He has prayed to have our curse revoked;
And, subtly, we must have a truce invoked
And seek the olive for his haunted life;
There's ever more to gain from peace than strife.   500
So, ascend and call them back to me – recall
Them, yes, the Faithfuls, one and all,
Now that morning struts the sky with light
And draws the daylight ever near to sight;
I shall wait to meet them all with you,
And bring their minds to know a higher view;
The man is pardoned, and do tell them why:
Sometimes to sin is not to have to die.'[21]
Speaking thus, and pointing to the earth,
The monarch took a deep (and deeper) breath;   510
Then he pitched the youngster out of sight
With a fiery blast of air to aid his flight.

*   *   *

---

[20] Glorious Word: Scripture. See also 'Holy Book' (I. 536)
[21] The line is rather antithetical to 'The soul who sins shall die.' (Ezekiel 18:20, NKJV).

Now, among the Faithfuls, yes, the five,
The voice of Axe would brashly come alive:
'One of us must think himself as smart
As some votary of the Sophists' art
That commends the obvious bad as good,
And paints the good as hardly understood.
But wiser than sophistic, as you know,
Wiser, yes, in many ways that show,   520
Must one brook a row whose sure reward
Is lose our focus to some queer discord?
He's the sovereign of the worlds' unwise
That argues with a fool that thinks he's wise.
So I'm bound to ignore his rash offence
And face the object of his doomed defence.
Like a jury, we must show the man
The sternest, scariest faces that we can,
And probe his conscience with that quaint device
That's known to keep his dubious kind from lies.   530
An oath, I mean, will make a liar sway
And bind him to the truth he's loath to say.
And though, as said, he learnt to lie from birth,
And he's the bravest liar known on earth,
I've hatched a worthy plot to trap the spook:[22]
He'll swear by heaven and our Holy Book.
We'll trap him with an oath that's strong and grim,
And which is sure to wring the truth from him.'

          *   *   *

And brashly did Machete answer back,
As if to say 'my wits are far from slack'.   540

---

[22] The spook: a sarcastic allusion to the author.

And this was what (in quick reply) he said,
As he gently scratched and shook his head:
'I'll sooner give my mind its quietus
Than yield to such a dubious afflatus
That thinks that humans will reveal the truth
With lies encrusted on their earliest tooth.
And let the deepest furrows ring our eyes,
I'll still be wary to think we are wise.'
And he paused and bared his hairy chest,
And quickly went ahead to tell the rest: 550
'Of men and oaths and lying we must know
And cease to let our cocky wisdom crow;
That, though they face a threat of injury,
Their liars' tongues incline to perjury;
But their truthful ones will tell, perforce,
The truth that oaths or threats cannot enforce.
So if, indeed, a man has lied from birth,[23]
And is the bravest liar known on earth,
Then no oath will do to sway his throat,
For liars lie the freer under oath.'   560
Speaking thus, he brought his voice to rest,
And clasped his arms across his hairy chest.

*   *   *

And Sword would banter, with a knowing smile,
'Some agile PATRIOT (for some SCUD) missile!'[24]
And smiling, whistling, like a happy ranger,
He pulled apart and whispered to Avenger:
'A gold shield for a silver thrust of wit!'

---

[23] Compare I. 557-558 with I. 533-534.
[24] PATRIOT and SCUD missiles were deployed during Gulf War I.

And both, unmindful of their happy fit,
Staggered with delirium, uncontrolled,
Forward, backwards, from their troubled fold.   570

　　　*　　　*　　　*

　It was Doom who, now, with hints of pain,
Tried to check the Faithfuls' deepening strain.
'You, and you,' he poked two mates to ask,
'Are you truly glad to stall our task?
And you, and you,' he poked the other two,
'Do you laugh and giggle, quack and coo,
And not see the grievous wrong of those
Whose rows betray the canker in our rose?
I mean our envied rose of unity,
That hides some canker of disunity.'   580
Doom, the Faithful, paused; and then he said,
With bile and venom swirling in his head:
'From now till success let our feuds be mum;
Success: when we've seized that haughty scum;
The scum: the man that threatens all of us,
By whose scrawny neck must hang our curse,
Our curse, our monarch's unrelenting spell,
That's rendered him a candidate for hell.'
Here, he drew the curtain on his speech,
Happy with its more-than-aural reach,   590
While a veil of silence wrapped them all,
As the anger simmered in his skull.

Canto II

*Reason, a sovereign of an
extraterrestrial, sublunary
kingdom, having heard and
considered the author's plea for
his intervention, sends five of his
subjects, the Stalwarts, to thwart
the Faithfuls' plan; whereupon
the Stalwarts leave their kingdom
for the earth to carry out his
command, and other related
occurrences.*

On his throne that mingles with the sky,
Reason sits to watch the clouds float by;
In his plateau, bordered by the sky,
Reason sits to watch the moon slide by.

* * *

Now, the author's plea had reached his ears,
A plea that dripped with anguish and with tears;
And Reason, yes, had pondered through a plan
To take help to the joy-forsaken man.
And worried, he would wonder in his heart:
'Can deed and longing dwell so far apart,   10
That those who pray for pardon from above
Won't forgive, or share their stake in love?'
And having scanned a stretch of rocky ground,

He raised his eyes and turned it round and round,
And, calling on some aides that numbered five,
His voice, as calm as measured, came alive:
'When their hour of vengeance shall arrive,
Then, I know, our five shall match their five.'[25]
And now he felt some soreness in his voice,
And cleared his throat, and held his words by choice;   20
Then, to address the five – with heightened poise –
He unbarred the portal to his inner voice:
'You'll go to extend our influence and our reach,
And fight off an unheard felonious breach;
That, to indulge his hard hubristic head,
A mortal dared to curse his like for dead.'
And Reason paused to rouse the five's acclaim,
And, pointing down and earthward, ordered them:
'Now, descend and thwart the rising five[26]
Who go as one to take our friend alive,   30
And then invoke their worse-than-fatal curse
To crush his soul – whose sole resort is us.
And though the earth is mired in apathy,
Should we shun his plea for sympathy
And leave him in the lurch, who loved our ways,
Though a faithful, from his infant days?'
And Reason paused, he paused his speech again,
And resumed speaking, but with mounting strain:
'With their arrow having left the bow,
And flying forth to do the work of woe,   40
Our best resort is shield their human aim
(The very object of their rightful blame)

---

[25] Our five: the Stalwarts. Their five (likewise in II. 228): the Faithfuls.
[26] The rising five: the Faithfuls – 'rising' to the earth from their subterranean kingdom.

Or yet divert the arrow, while on course,
And disincline our feelings from remorse.'
And he paused, and went ahead to speak,
His voice rebounding from a rocky peak:
'Here – my backing – it is strong and firm!
Yes, you have my backing, I affirm!
You, my Stalwarts and my liberal kind;
And our counter goal is thus outlined: 50
We must neither brook their spiteful spell,
Nor have the soul of Zumba dragged to hell.'

*   *   *

Having heard their king, the stalwart five,
Eager, yes, to keep their friend[27] alive,
Left their king and kingdom for the earth,
To find and keep him from the reach of death.
No sooner than they'd left their high abode
Did zealous Stone brandish his verbal goad:
'Mine is not a heart to shrink from war
Or flinch before a running stream of gore.   60
Nor do I house a squeamish heart in me
That'll survey the clash ahead and flee.
Mine's a heart well-seasoned to succeed
At the task our king has just decreed,
The task to go and battle with their side,[28]
Who seem to deem us asses for their ride.'
And he paused, and went ahead to speak
(That leading Stalwart with a streak
Of bile, and the temper of a fer-de-lance):

---

[27] Their friend: a reference to the author.
[28] Their side: a reference to the Faithfuls.

'How they tread their mazy rounds[29], and prance,　　　70
And wend their ways in whorls towards their ruin,
Their five, to enforce our loyal friend's undoing!
And how their long and sooty torches glow
To singe him well, before the blaze below.'[30]
And he rubbed his bleary eyes, and said
(His stumpy fingers scratching at his head):
'Need I wonder that their ways are whorled,
Though they issue from the underworld?'
Thus, he aired the words that came his way,
That boulder full of fury, you might say.　　　80

　　　*　　　*　　　*

　Panther, next to Stone, would roar aloud
(His eyes as sullen as a stormy cloud):
'A mighty lion with a shaggy mane,
I'm happy that I go to be their bane,
That I'll bring their retributive end,
A sudden end, before they reach our friend.'
And he paused, and went ahead to say
(His eyes now focused on their downward way):
'Down and earthwards, let us, yes, descend
And bring their[31] mission to a futile end.　　　90
Let's go, with hurry, and repel their curse
That trails the author who is yet for us.
How they mean to spite our throne above
Who seek to ruin the author whom we love!
To ignore the offence their pride can give

---

[29] The phrase 'mazy round' occurs in Alexander Pope's *Essay on Man*.
[30] The blaze below: the fire of Hell.
[31] Their (likewise in II. 108): a reference to the Faithfuls.

Is to give the lie to why we live.'
And Panther paused again, he paused again,
And went on speaking with a little strain
(But not before he'd gently raise his eyes,
Raise his eyes towards the stormy skies,   100
Nor before he'd lower them yet again,
Lower them to that sloping-steep terrain):
'I have seen the portent in the skies,
Seen it with my sharper inner eyes,
The portent of a mottled sky, and grey,
And ravens cawing for a bloody day;
So brace up for a battle most sanguine,
And let's exact some glory from their ruin.'
And he paused again, and thumped his chest;
And went on speaking, speaking to the rest:[32]   110
'And I shall be the leader of our squad,
The first to sink their weapons in their blood.
My lion is the kind whose distant roar
Neither man nor spirit can ignore,
And those our rivals must rethink their aim,
Or face the danger that my snarls proclaim.'
Thus, he said the much he had to say,
Pointing at his "mottled sky, and grey".[33]

*   *   *

And Care, the cautious, was the next to speak,
His voice as mild as ever, and as weak: 120
'Why assert our doubtful luck, and grin,
And pretend we're truly sure to win?

---

[32] 'The rest' of the Stalwarts.
[33] 'Mottled…grey': see II. 105, 118 and 134.

Don't we know that, with a flash of hate,
Some peevish god may thwart a cheerful fate,
Or luck contrive to foil triumphal dreams,
Just to indulge her vain and prankish whims.
Please ask tetchy fortune what she feels,
And seek the favour of her spinning wheels,
Lest her distaff, as its thread unwinds,
Weave confusion to our eager minds.   130
Who knows what the stars intend for us:
Shame or honour? Glory or remorse?
Shouldn't we rather wait awhile and pray
Beneath our lion's "mottled sky, and grey"
Than hasten forward and proclaim our right
To win a war whose sense is far from sight?'
Here the Stalwart with a cautious bent,
Pursed his lips in scorn and – fell silent.

                    *   *   *

  Bluff, the gutsy, was the next to speak
(He called himself the never-tongue-in-cheek),   140
And these, I recall, were the things he said,
As he wrung his hands and wagged his head:
'It's the will – the winner in all things –
That makes us slaves of fate or makes us kings.
It's the weak that whimsy luck deters;
The strong defy the verdict of the stars.
The ablest sailor tames the wildest wave;
Fortune yields her bounties to the brave.
Know: the gifts of heaven honour strain,
And let misfortune dog your steps in vain.   150
Never will your good luck toe the line,

If your will must waver, or decline.'
And Bluff, the gutsy, would observe a pause,
And resume speaking, but with lesser force:
'But such digressions undermine our stake,
Seeing that it's war we go to make.
So let's have our willing crew descend
And bring our rivals to a futile end;
And don't permit your zeal to sneak away,
Nor let your ardent love of glory sway.'   160

*   *   *

That was all that gutsy Bluff could say,
Before the voice of Smithy led the way;
And feeling less enthused than ill at ease,
Smithy made to give his thoughts release
(Speaking, as he'd put it, 'to enhance
Their ways who cast their lot with will or chance'.
It was to Bluff and Care he addressed each word,
Which sent a shiver down his vocal cord):
'That will and chance have jointly shaped my lot
Makes me think your row will come to naught.   170
Besides, I marvel at the strange mistake
That thinks it's truly war we go to make.
Perhaps our eyes are not equipped to see
A mission steeped in ambiguity;
And how that fortune will indeed be odd,
For which we'll sink their weapons in their blood;[34]
We go to wage a war – as said – unarmed[35]

---

[34] Compare with II. 112.
[35] The speaker alludes to the contradicting fact that they, the Stalwarts, are unarmed, though supposedly war-bound.

And think we'll truly leave the fray unharmed,
And fight victorious till the very end.
On what do such illusory hopes depend?   180
To what, I wonder, do they trace their root?
And what (if not our rout) shall be their fruit?'
And Smithy waited on his words awhile,
And went on speaking with a hazy smile:
'We still may buckle, though we lose our pride,
And though the right were truly on our side,
And though, indeed, our cause were truly just,
And though we're right to see war as a must.
For, yes, the book is known to all of us,
That stung our rivals and provoked their curse.   190
We've heard of treachery and of blasphemy,
And more that'll make a friend an enemy.
We go to right a wrong, and negotiate
A path of honour with an angered faith.'[36]
And he paused again, and went ahead,
Speaking calmly, as he shook his head:
'And though I have the will to face their five,
And help our protégé to stay alive,
I'll rather urge their anger, just but high,
To view his error with a lenient eye.'   200
This was all he said, the lot indeed,
Before Panther's voice resumed the lead.

*   *   *

And Panther, first, would mutter an aside:
'I? To play the coward? Lose my pride?
Stay transfixed – a totem in disgrace?

---

[36] Faith: see footnote number 2.

And simply watch them kill to spite my face?
Oh heaven, heaven, liquidate the thought
That my lion's strength may come to naught.
Damn the thought that says my might may fail,
That my lion's strength may not avail.   210
I'll always tell the coward (as the brave):
The path of caution leads but to the grave.[37]
And though I have no amour for my chest,
I shall still subject my strength to test;
I shall rise above this creeping fear,
Though I march without a sling or spear.
Nor having bows, nor arrows, nor a shield,
Shall stall my descent to some earthly field
Where I'll fight to vindicate our cause
To save a man whose faith is hinged on us.'   220
And he paused, and calmly went ahead,
Speaking, as he shook his shaggy head:
'Yes, I think the right should win, unharmed,
Plagued to war by error[38], though unarmed.
There are hidden arms the just may have,
Deadlier than the arrow and the stave;[39]
Thus armed, comrades, let's march to the earth,
And, bare-hand, bring their five to ruin and death;
Let's march to the earth, the realm of men,
To dare some painted devil in his den.'   230
That was all he said, or had to say,
All he added on their downward way.

---

[37] With the substitution of 'caution' with 'honour', the line would read exactly like an epigram in Thomas Gray's 'Elegy Written in a Country Churchyard'.
[38] Error: wrong.
[39] Stave: bow.

*　　*　　*

And Stone, the zealous, straining hard and taut,
Raised his voice and thundered in support:
'The devil is a bull with horns of clay,
Good to grip and break without delay,
A mighty lion merely for his roar,
A toothless, pawless[40] grizzly, lame and hoar;
In vain his powers haunt the powerless,
That quintessence of sham and nothingness!'　　　　240
And he paused, and went ahead to say
(More than keen to go the lion's way):
'Let's firmly fix our minds on glory still,
The glory that must not elude our will.
We must fix our minds on martial fame,
Though we attain it in the midst of blame.'
He paused again, and raised his nostrils high
(Flaring like a bullock's) to the sky,
And shook his head, and pawed the ground below,
And neighed and grunted, raring – yes – to go:　　　　250
'To war, to war, to glory or to death,
To leave our presence rooted in the earth!'

*　　*　　*

And Care, the cautious, and the next in line,
Answered with a shudder down his spine:
'Shouldn't it be foolish – irrational – to dare
The armed with hands as frail as bare?'
And he paused, and licked his mottled tongue,

---

[40] Pawless: without paws.

And then allowed his voice to roll along:
'Indeed, I'm willing to refrain from talking,
As I am to stop my feet from walking: 260
To wait here, idle, limp and battle-shy,
Till our quest is backed with arms supply.
I'm embittered – I have been for long –
To think we'll go to war to right a wrong,
Whereas there is still before our eyes
The prospect of a moral compromise.'
And to roundly make his pungent mark,
He ended with this sleight-of-tongue remark:
'And that impression seems an awful thing,
That right can be the first to use the sling.'   270

          *   *   *

    Bluff, the Stalwart at the back of Care,
Had some nagging thoughts of his to share,
As, pointing to the ground, with every stride,
He voiced his backing for the martial side:
'They take the horns by the bull – the brave –
And dread no descent – even to the grave.
And many a valiant fighter, sure, disarms
The fiercest bull for all its horny arms.
It's no assured advantage to be armed;
Nor must they lose that go to war unarmed;   280
Call to mind the towering warrior-king
Felled like lumber by the rustic sling:
The great Goliath, with his shield and spear,
Stood no ground with David from the rear.
Should we say he's armed who, with a sling,
Dethrones a dreaded armour-fitted king,

And claims his body that has kissed the dust,
And sends his men stampeding as they must?
The stripling, David, left that fray unharmed.
Should we say the lad was truly armed?   290
He went home to become and – all along –
Has been a gem of honour, pomp and song.
So march on, onward, to the earth (in sight),
And win such honour to our king's delight.
I pledge to be the first to dare their five,
And strip their armour, bare-hand and alive.
Yes, I'm more than eager for that fray,
At which our lion means to take a prey.'
Thus, the words he uttered (long or brief?),
That would bring his anxious heart relief.   300
It also brought his martial pride relief
To say their crew would never come to grief.

*   *   *

    And silent Smithy gave in to the urge
To work the bellows of his vocal forge,
As the reins of speech returned to him.
He levelled censure at 'that vaunting whim,
The boastful whim that's prompted some of us
To make war seem our first and last recourse,
And yet our only option in-between,
To make it seem we're truly sure to win.   310
March on, though unarmed, they urge us all,
And crave our full obedience to their call,
Our full obedience, though towards the grave,
And there await the man we seek to save.
I'll sooner, yes, renounce the rest of us,

Than come to see war as our sole recourse;
Such a war we're sure to win unarmed
And – how like David! – leave the fray unharmed.'[41]
And he paused, and coolly went ahead,
Speaking, as he shook and shook his head   320
(Some weighty grief would lie around his chest,
As his rolling voice addressed the rest[42]):
'It numbs my head and, yes, appals me too,
That souls with learning think like some of you.
Should I blame this descent to the earth:
Where the wise may meet a foolish death,
Where the light of thought is ever dim,
Where folly, yes, is said to reign supreme,
Where shepherd-doubt and all his rambling flock,
Are ever stumbling on some stump of luck;   330
Where the heads of truths, for all their cries,
May ever end up on the block of lies,
Like the very truth that war is pain,
A perverse route to glory in the main!'
And he paused again, and went ahead,
Having brought to rest his anxious head:
'And let me set our errant views aright,
And rend the veil that blurs our inner light:
Our furious call to arms will come to naught,
Since our sovereign only fights with thought;   340
Yes, Reason only cares to fight with thought:
Ideas are all with which he's ever fought,
The weapons he has mastered through and through,
And would approve for use by me – and you.
And don't forget that we're his true elect,

---

[41] Compare with II. 289.
[42] The rest: the rest of the Stalwarts.

Not as much for brawn as intellect.
And so our lion does not flinch in vain,
That's said to seek some prey to blood his den.
Yes, I know our king; I know him well;
And your warlike hearts must cease to swell;   350
For soon his orders will annul the fray
And tame our lion's urge to take a prey.
So seek caution and apply the brakes
To this *intention* to reduce our stakes,
To reduce our stakes from talk to strife,
And put at greater risk our author's life.'
And having said the much he had to say,
He allowed another voice to lead the way.

                    *   *   *

And Care, the cautious, having stretched a sigh,
Said to Smithy – in direct reply: 360
'I deem it odd – your incredulity
That deems a learned fool an oddity,
And more than odd – your undisguised surprise
To know the learned can be quite unwise.
Think of wisdom in a learned mule;
A fool that's sent to school remains a fool.'

                    *   *   *

Now, retired to his marble throne,
A sobered Reason pondered all alone:
'Yes, my orders, of its safe purport?
To think I've lent the right a wrong support   370
And, tactless, fanned the smouldering flames of strife,

Though talk may yet redeem our author's life.'
And, sliding down the slope of afterthought,
The pensive sovereign mumbled, as he thought:
'But, yet, a tepid joy may warm my mood,
And turn my hopes from very bad to good,
To think my Stalwarts should return unharmed,
Having left our plateau-realm unarmed.
But then,' as yet inclined to afterthought,
But sliding to a darker shade of thought,   380
Darker for its hue and depth and strain,
The sobered sovereign pondered yet again:
'Should they, my Stalwarts, come under attack,
What becomes the import of their lack,
Their lack of tools of warfare, as it were?
And what becomes their shield against the spear?
Can they meet the five[43] and go unharmed,
Or hope to foil the threat they pose unarmed?'
His mind, adrift and nervous, half-controlled,
Would soon return within his firmer hold,   390
Though not before he'd summon his courier,
A page with springy steps, whose ear was near,
And who would soon be standing before him,
His boyish visage looking tense and grim.
     And Reason, mildly ruffled, subtly sad,
Wrung his moist hands, as he told the lad:
'Go down to the earth without delay,
Down our plateau by the easiest way,
To seek our Stalwarts – gone to take relief
To a worthy friend of ours immersed in grief: 400
A man whom faith has branded writ profane,
And has dispatched a crew to be his bane;

---

[43] The five: the Faithfuls.

And though he was in error, I admit,
We're obliged to seek his benefit
And win just pardon for his haunted life,
And win it soon, without recourse to strife.'
Reason paused, and then said to the boy
(Raring now to go, as if with joy):
'Now proceed, descend towards the earth,
To those I sent to thwart the five from faith,	410
The five that faith has sent to fetch our friend,
And bring his sweet life to a bitter end.
They number five like faith's opposing crew,
And may be near to reach, though out of view;
Recall them from their mission, unfulfilled; for
A plan unfolds in me, not vile as war,
To save our friend, our errant friend, from death,
And yet augment the strength of peace on earth.'
Speaking thus, he turned the swivel throne,
Wheeled it off, and left the lad alone.	420
And soon the lad was earthbound with his word
Whom our author called his 'chosen lord'[44].

*   *   *

Now lift your voice; lift your voice and say;
Your voice, not mine, must rise and lead the way:
What now transpired among the rising five[45]
Who wished our author more dead than alive?
What – the thought – that, of its own accord,
Changed their common tilt towards discord?
A love as yet profound inspires my choice

[44] His 'chosen lord' (also 'my chosen lord' in I. 250): a reference to Reason.
[45] The rising five: A reference to the Faithfuls. See footnote number 26.

To be the human echo of your voice.   430

*   *   *

Now they climbed towards the unguarded gate
That opens to the earth – a medial state
(A realm of muddled wise-and-foolish haunts
That's heaven, hell, purgatory, all at once;
A boundless, timeless prison of the free
Chained to grief and, worse, mortality;
Bounty's home where lack remains the norm,
Exposed to every wind and every storm;
And where, as said, the hapless multitude
Are preys to evil though they seek the good,   440
And the few whose lot may seem the best
Are neither quite the happiest nor at rest.
The earth, I dare say, is a curious place,
And often out of sync with sense and grace.
Or what explains such marvel of disgrace[46]

---

[46] The events alluded to from II. 445-454 are the same that Chinua Achebe
describes on page 248 of *There Was a Country, a Personal History of Biafra*
(2012, the Penguin edition), as '… some real events that occurred during
Nigeria's Fourth Republic (circa 2004), during which the very opposite of
the democratic ideal was at work,' and then explains: 'Anambra State, the
past home of several venerated Nigerians, such as Nnamdi Azikiwe, the
Okigbo brothers – Pius and Christopher – Kenneth Dike, and others – was
literally and figuratively on fire. There was a succession of events during a
tussle for political power that resulted in renegades arresting a sitting
governor and buildings being ransacked and burned to the ground by
hoodlums – those infamous rent-a-crowd hooligans at the beck and call of
corrupt politicians with plenty of money but very low IQs …' Incidentally,
this allusion precedes Achebe's publication of his aversion to the events in
the book, though the aversion was apparent from his previous utterances and
well-publicised protest letter rejecting a national honour from a Nigerian

That an unlettered scum dares to outpace
The minds of many a learned man,
Strive and run with him the best they can?
Or ask our dear Nigerians, if you please,
To give a meaning to this siege of fleas;   450
Ask, I mean, our great Anambrarians[47],
Once captives of a prince of barbarians;
Ask them why they only seemed to wince
Or cringe before that drab and puny prince.
Some thought Abacha's[48] end was such relief;
I ponder what they thought and wince in grief;
For such misrule has simply changed its cloth
That turns sweet power to a poisoned broth –
Served across our land[49] by every brat
Who can boast to be a 'democrat'.   460
Besides tyranny, there's a lot to fix,
A lot like spreading cracks in moulded bricks,
A lot to fix about our crumbling state,
A lot to fix to avert a grievous fate.
May some great soul rise up to the task
To raze this evil with a rotten mask
And reclaim our faith – deservingly –
In our dear nation and her destiny.)
    Mumbling, on their knees, they crossed their chests,
And brushed some dusty threshold with their breasts;   470
Then, and briskly, they would stand erect,

---

president he regarded as the mastermind of those unsavoury happenings.
[47] Anambrarians: the people of Anambra State in southeastern Nigeria.
[48] General Sani Abacha (1943-1998): Nigerian military ruler who died in office.
[49] Our land (likewise 'our crumbling state' in ll. 463 and 'our nation' in ll. 468): a reference to the poet's country, Nigeria.

Clap together, shout, and genuflect,
And then return to standing on their feet.
All these they did and, yes, with one repeat,
And then proceeded past some passageway
That led into the earth, without delay;
But not before their leader, Doom, would scrawl
Some lines in cursive in the sight of all[50];
Yes, he scrawled them in a slanted hand;
Beside that entrance point he let them stand: 480
'Here lives the man whose being is split in two:
Half-god; half-human; and half-spirit, too.
His pride is all vain, and he's here to tell,
For he's whole as nothing, and he knows it well.'

*   *   *

    With the threshold well behind the crew,
And a new and shining dawn in view,
Doom (the one in front) began to speak
(His voice was jerky, and his tone was weak,
As, with caution brewing in his mind,
He addressed the other Faithfuls right behind):   490
'Friends, its self-deception that we smile
With rancour spreading in our rank and file;
We're better off to reach a quick accord
And bind our purpose with a common cord
Than keep on moving while yet at a loss
How to treat the man that bears our curse.'
And he paused and gently stroked his head
(That grumpy soul, the Faithfuls' arrowhead),
Then, proceeding with a hint of force,

---

[50] All: a reference to the Faithfuls as a group.

He turned his speech around, and stated thus: 500
'You think he's alone, with no defence,
The man we go to tackle his offence:
You think there's no bone behind his back,
The man we hope to waste upon the rack?'
And he paused and stroked his head again,
And went on speaking with a little strain:
'But how can we conclude this work of strife
With triumph, and without the loss of life?'

         *   *   *

Trudging on, his voice would follow next,
Avenger's voice (the grumpiest of the rest[51]):   510
'Thoughts like Doom's had also crossed my mind,
But their forms were hazy, undefined;
For, come to weigh his words for sanity,
They fight to win who fight in unity;
But dissent ruins a war on every front,
And rancour is an army's heaviest brunt.'
And he paused, and went on with his speech,
And, speaking, amplified his tonal reach:
'But then, about the object of our goal,
Our final purpose for the author's soul: 520
Let's find the treachery in its mute conceit,
And then resolve on what to do with it.'

         *   *   *

And another (Sword) would speak his due,
His voice the weakest (of the risen crew[52]);

---

[51] The rest: the rest of the Faithfuls, excluding Doom, the last speaker.

And, in sum and substance, he agreed
To give his 'due support to any deed',
And mumbled: 'I agree with what was said,'
That 'peace is vital to a fruitful raid.'

*　　*　　*

And Machete was the next to speak;
And his voice, like Sword's, was flat and weak:　　　530
'The more I crave a path that dignifies,
The more I wish our mission clarifies:
What's his ultimate lot – death of life?
Do I just proceed to use my knife
Once he's near the icy reach of death,
And slice him off the surface of the earth,
As a fitting gesture of reproof,
And one that'll give the earth the needed proof
That our faith, indeed, was built[53] on peace,
Peace enough to keep all men at ease?　　　540
Yes, must I ignore his mien of guilt,
Should he come before my brazen hilt?
Should I, though he bows before my blade,
Proceed to slice away his learned head?'

*　　*　　*

Axe became the very next to speak;
And, like Sword's, his voice was flat and weak:
'Yes, the man in question caused offence,

---

[52] The risen crew: the Faithfuls, having now 'risen' to the earth from their subterranean kingdom.
[53] See footnote number 18.

To our faith, and death's the comeuppance,
Hence we seek a cross to hoist him high,
And roast his rebel spirit in the sky;   550
But I deem the grim intention strange:
Should a moral faith exact revenge?
A tooth for a tooth, you know, my chums,
Will leave all with bleeding, toothless gums.
An eye for an eye, as Gandhi said,
Will leave two blinded eyes on every head.
Of all the victories we may yet enact,
The worthiest one should leave his life intact,
Though our action shouldn't negate the word
Of he who governs with an iron sword.[54]   560

And though our pain is worse for his conceit,
To kill him is to triumph in defeat.'
Thus their final speaker spoke his due,
To sway the members of their risen crew.

*   *   *

You whose guidance is my greatest joy,
I press – not to pester and annoy;
But tell me, of the five that Reason sent,
How their course of vengeance would be bent.
Or let me trace the progress of their course
That would veer off from the use of force.   570

*   *   *

Care was now the first to make a speech:

---

[54] Compare with I. 92.

'How victory must remain beyond our reach!
Torn by dissent and a wordy strife,
Will our dear friend not forfeit his life?
Be sure he slides towards the end with haste,
And learn to view our rancour with distaste.'
And he paused, and breathed hard and deep,
And went on speaking, as if half-asleep
(No, his voice it was that seemed to drowse,
For all the passions that it meant to douse):   580

'Should we, bare-hand, dare their[55] spears and knives,
And, doing so, be inclined to lose our lives,
And expose our friend to perils worse than dire:
A death without a coffin, grave or pyre,
Ground to bare dust by a hostile might,
When we've lost a worse-than-groundless fight?'
He paused again, and went ahead to ask,
And, asking, bring to an end his vocal task:
'And shouldn't a firm decision bind our crew,
And string us to some common goal in view?'   590

       *   *   *

   And Panther gently cracked his neck, and sighed,
And sighed and sighed again, and then replied
(As, all around, he saw the others smile, and
Take the last known speaker by the hand):
'Why opt to walk the path of cowardice,
And yield my pliant ears to squeamish lies?
It's still the deviant, in their compromise,
That shrink from fighting – for a fighter dies.

---

[55] Their: a reference to the Faithfuls.

Fear must not derail our sense of right;
The strongest darkness fears the weakest light.'   600

And he paused and sighed, and sighed again,
And went on speaking (with a hint of pain):
'Must we view renown with such regret
That, alarmed, we tremble and forget
That they err who shrink from risk and loss?
Who must wear the crown must bear the cross.'
Again, he paused, and coolly went ahead,
Speaking, as he shook his shaggy head:
'Of what is said, I still must put in front
The brave but risky option to confront[56];   610

We must cease to waste our precious breath,
Or babble till our friend is put to death.
I will yield to subterfuge, or fight,
Once our resolution comes to light:
To make our friend (of every curious stunt)
The single object of a double hunt,
Or join to drive his stalkers all away,
If our will may cease to flag and sway.
I move to stage a ballot right away,
And let the greater voters have their way.'   620

*   *   *

And the others, lacking words to waste,
Called out for the ballot – 'and with haste!
Swifter goes the flight of time,' they said,
'And swifter yet may come the crucial raid,

---

[56] To confront the Faithfuls.

The crucial raid to quench the very man
Whom we seek to shelter, while we can.'
    The hairy hands they raised to vote were four
(Four-to-one) against the choice of war;
And sworn against that option they went all
To protect Zumba from a fatal fall.   630

Canto III

*A disagreement, having ensued
among the Faithfuls, persists;
whereupon they break into two
factions, one of which encounters
the Stalwarts and, being armed,
unlike them, easily overpowers
them and takes them hostage,
threatening to keep them in
captivity until they are ransomed
with the author, and other related
occurrences.*

And the one but two-fold search began:
To seize with doubt or save a threatened man.

*   *   *

    With a cheerless mien, a heart in gloom,
Our pensive author paced his hidden room.
In his solitude, his lonely bind,
A stream of worries gurgled through his mind.
In-between the cramps, his lips, the air,
Rustled as he mumbled his despair:
'O endless pall of gloom! O joyless night!
That yields no hope for dawn's returning light.'   10
The twin, sepulchral laments thus exhumed,
He observed a pause and, mumbling yet, resumed:

'And how endure the new and sadder curse,
A man's sworn partner who has fled for worse
And, proving true her vow to die his crutch,
Left her crippled husband in the lurch?'[57]
Now his eyes were glazed, his gazes blanks,
A copious rash of sweating blanched his flanks;
And his mind, his thoughts, his words (their sense),
Had shed much weight (in terms of coherence);   20
And (lost in thought) he mumbled yet again
(His heart was heavy, weighted down with pain):
'Two slanted paths, before my inner eye,
Rise to bridge the solid earth and sky,
With their flaming pillars lengthening well,
Well beyond the darkest pit of hell.'
Which vision brought our author to reflect,
Reflect upon its meaning – in effect:
'Are these the flaming paths of death in view?
And of courage – drenched in fire too?   30
Should I then be bold to take my life,
And live as haunted in the afterlife?
Or yet, to endure a toil without relief,
And raise eternal monuments to grief?'
But such clouding of his soul was brief:
Life will bring no grief without relief;
And a mind distressed may yet prefer
To cling to hope and repudiate despair.
And our author (seeing a shaft of light)
Would rethink his dark and knotty plight: 40
'But can't there be such allusive clues
Beneath this tangled yarn of faith's misuse,

---

[57] III. 13-16: the author laments his desertion by his wife after the monarch
called for his head (see I. 23-24, then I. 31-32).

That I may, through this sacrificial pain,
Dislodge restrictions to the minds of men?'
And soon our author drifted off to sleep,
In the loosening clutch of worry's grip.
   To track a vision through his slumbering mind
Is a task we mustn't leave behind;
To unveil a dream he had, and maybe more,
Is a task we'd rather not ignore;   50
Yes, a task we'd rather not bypass,
As we explore his worse-than-grievous pass.

        *   *   *

   It was a dream about the monarch's crew
Moving snake-wise, slithering into view,
About the Faithfuls, yes, the monarch's five,
Winding sideways, with an onward drive:
A moving zigzag of curiosity,
Thrusting forward with velocity.
Zumba saw them, though his eyes were closed,
And all his senses more than full-reposed;   60
He saw them in his somnolence, his sleep,
Which had passed from deep to very deep,
And then to trancelike slumber and to such
That hangs the mind beyond the reach of touch.

        *   *   *

   And Axe, the last of them, was heard to say:
'Friends, begin the search without delay;
Find the farthest caves and probe within
For he whose hopes may hide in them unseen;

Comb the forests, make the mountains plain[58],
Though the man, when found, may not be slain.   70
How good – the bitter law of sweet revenge!
How better still – the grace that fosters change!'
And now he held his tinny voice in check;
And went on, having cracked his sturdy neck:
'I pledge to lead our mission through the earth
To find the man we're charged to bring to death,
For whom our master, I remain convinced,
Will douse the holy fury thus evinced.
Hence, good comrades, let us march along
Towards the mid-ground of reward and wrong: 80
Where justice should reverse the author's dent,
But make sure he outlasts the incident,
And so restore in full his righteous bent
With every scope to live the lessons learnt.
Thus, the author, should we truly win,
Must survive our urge to clear his sin;
So firmly tread the ground with all your paws,
Much like lions, but with sheathed claws.
Else, must we endorse the fears on earth,
And vindicate our faith with blood and death?[59]'   90
And having said the much he had to say,
He allowed another voice to lead the way.

*   *   *

---

[58] Plain: bare.

[59] This intervention by Axe (especially in the light of the attitude reflected in I. 67-70, then I. 72-94) signals a new disposition to the author and the monarch's call for his head on the part of the Faithfuls, which in turn may be regarded as indicative of the transformation of the speaker from an extremist to a moderate. The rightness of this new disposition is contested by Doom, the next speaker.

And Doom was the next our author heard,
Though his mind, you'd say, was drowsy-eared.
This – the much he added, on their way,
Eager, just like Axe, to have his say:
'Friends, I think his rays were aimed astray
Who pledged to lead us – down a curious way?
Who voiced a wish to be our leading light,
To light our pathway – to the obscure right?'   100
And he paused, and coolly went ahead
(Scratching gently at his roundish head):
'The very charge we have is well defined;
But I'll more than gladly calm my mind
Which, angry at the author's rude challenge,
Is throbbing with the venom of revenge,
The vengeance-venom sure to freeze his blood
And end his learned life to please our lord.
I'll nod in assent to who seemed to say
That greater good is bound to come our way   110
Should we all forgive and spare the man,
And give him scope to thrive as, yes, we can.
But who compared the worth of tit for tat
With that of mercy might have erred at that,
Whose aim, I reckon, was to trap our sense
With the cunning of his eloquence.
Or, are we resolved to so forgive
As his light would lead us to believe?
Or yet, to storm the earth with one accord
And vindicate our faith with death and blood[60]?'   120
And having duly said the much he could,
He let deflate his broad, venomous hood.

---

[60] The line echoes III. 90.

*   *   *

Now the monarch's page was visible,
A floating silhouette, discernible,
And our author saw him in his dream:
A fleeting shadow, lifelike and agleam,
Racing hard to meet the risen crew
Sooner than he'd floated into view.
And he raised his fruity voice and called,
Called out to the five he'd have recalled;   130
This was what the message bearer said
To the Faithfuls – not so far ahead;
This, I recollect, was what he said,
Standing near the Faithfuls – in a shade:
'Please, listen to our master's other voice,
Pay attention to his better choice;
In error you have lingered to misjudge
And foster error with a moral urge:
The man you seek may truly not be killed
As our angered sovereign might have willed;   140
It's our king that says to tell you this,
And I'm sure you do not hear amiss:
The man is pardoned; and he stated why –
"Sometimes to sin is not to have to die,"[61]
And said he'd wait to welcome all of us;
He has, I declare, annulled his curse,
The furious curse he heaped upon the head
Of he who hurt our faith and later fled,
Whom you mean to bring some ghastly fate;
In short, to find and promptly liquidate.   150

[61] The line echoes I. 508.

Bear to reverse now the path you take,
Since our lord has overturned the stake,
Being inclined to spare the sinner's life
And pull you homewards from the brink of strife.
Yes, to put it all the more aright,
He envisions justice in another light,
And sends me up to you to make it known,
How beyond revenge his heart has grown!'
Thus, the message bearer said his all,
And put paid to his mission of recall[62].   160

*   *   *

And pensive Reason, on his throne, reclined,
Shared reflections with our author's mind.
These – the very thoughts the sovereign shared,
Shared with Zumba – dreaming and in bed:
'Why keep faith in such spurious benefit
That seems to conquer, though it courts defeat?
For she merely stoops – for all her wars –
That confronts reason by the use of force.
My wish: that man would gladly walk her ways,
And faith correct by virtue when he strays;   170
But this – her swift recourse to strife and arms –
Strips the bride that's faith of all her charms.'
And Reason dammed his stream of thought (awhile)
To observe the Faithfuls 'in their rank and file',
And seeing them 'marching to a pointless task',
He'd free the stream and, thinking loudly[63], ask:
'Were they ever this unmerciful

---

[62] ...'his mission of recall': see I. 501-502.
[63] ... 'thinking loudly': thinking aloud.

That profess God as ever-merciful?'
Then he swept a gaze across the earth,
As he muttered underneath his breath: 180
'Must they follow yet – as if aright –
A creed whose path is strewn with dynamite?'

*   *   *

Noble seeker who must go before,[64]
Do keep me with you and tell me more.
How, in response to the later news[65],
Would the Faithfuls later air their views?
How did they – by action and by word –
Receive that message from their sobered lord.
Homer thrilled your pinions with delights,
Virgil warmed your wings upon the heights;   190
You may yet rely upon my pen,
And 'fly victorious on the lips of men.'[66]
Thus addressed, they waited to confirm
Who the speaker was, and then his aim;
To ascertain that, true, their royal lord
(Through the page) had truly sent them word;
And that the page had spoken as was told,
Though they thought his manners overbold.
They waited, yes, unmoving – in a fix? –

---

[64] ...'go before' (go in front): lead (as may be contrasted with come behind: follow).

[65] ... 'the later news': the news of the author's absolution, as conveyed by the monarch's page (see III 143-144).

[66] ... 'fly victorious on the lips of men': the phrase is credited to Ennuis, arguably the first great Roman poet, on page 152 of L. P. Wilkinson's translation of *The Georgics* for Penguin Classics; it occurs in line 13 of Book Three of the translation.

Till he joined their crew, and made them six;   200
And, speaking, more unhurried, loud and clear,
He passed conviction down their every ear,
Dispelled misgivings from each Faithful's mind;
But freed from doubt, they became dis-aligned.
This was true for some of them, at least,
The strict, unbending bigots in their midst,
Whose thirst for vengeance had been so aroused
That their quest for it could not be doused.
Doused, perhaps it could – but just by word
Spoken by their absent sovereign lord[67],   210
And not his proxy, as that speaker[68] was,
Whose voice they'd listen to but not endorse.
To think their lord could 'interdict that curse'
And choose indeed to 'thwart' their 'glory' thus
Would rankle them the more – such rigid ones,
Whose passions overheat most religions.
But didn't a thicket yield a wonder ram
That kept a human victim free from harm?
I mean that rare provision that would save
The Root of Israel[69] from an early grave,   220
Or rather, being set atop a pyre,
A slit throat and a sacrificial fire.
How the force of life redeems its own
By ways as oft amazing as unknown!

                    *   *   *

Axe, the last, was now the first to speak;

---

[67] ... 'their absent sovereign lord': a reference to the monarch.
[68] ... 'that speaker': a reference to the monarch's page.
[69] 'The Root of Israel': a reference to Isaac (see Genesis 22: 1-14).

And his mood and mien were far from meek;
His voice had found a curious way with mirth,
And the four with whom he'd reached the earth.
And thus, with beaming eyes, he spoke aloud
(His tone was such you'd call unduly proud,   230
A tone whose stark, unfeeling arrogance
Was sure to startle and to give offence,
To prove offensive to the rest of them,
The Faithfuls, as he basked in self-acclaim
And – bent to flaunt himself as credible –
Proved himself far less reliable):
'This sudden sign of distant hopes realised
Should leave me more contented than surprised;
It should cause my joy to know no bounds,
To fill the earth with loud, hilarious sounds;   240
Louder, for the hopes were mauled by doubts,
And our sceptics – their contentious bouts!'
And he paused, and brashly went ahead,
With a rush of hubris to his head:
'And that our hunter who will not be tame
May commence to roam the earth for game;
As he who spoke against my earlier doubt[70]
May commence to prove himself devout:
To justify the fear that's numbed the earth
And serve faith as a harbinger of death.'   250
And he paused again, and went ahead,
With a rush of venom to his head:
'Damn his doubts and let the truth be known,
And let the souls in all the worlds be shown
The one true sovereign of their most unwise,

---

[70] … 'he who spoke against my earlier doubt': a reference to Doom (see III
93-122).

Their all-presumptuous fool that thinks he's wise,
As now it's obvious – as I had declared –
That the author may at last be spared;
He's so forgiven that our royal boss
(Through a proxy) has annulled his curse.'   260
These, I recall, were the things he said,
And then returned to silence, looking staid.
And thus their mended fences[71] might have gone,
Razed down by his tactless words of scorn
That left his crewmates wandering at the haze
Of his new, unguarded turn of phrase.

*   *   *

And, yes, the first to hasten with reply
Was Doom (with a long and rasping sigh);
These, I recall, were the things he said,
Which our dreaming author also heard: 270
'How, indeed, his dubious hopes are true
Whose sense of vindication taunts our crew!
And who can doubt the wisdom of his type
That'll pluck the fruit of victory though unripe?'[72]
And he paused, and stretched a longer sigh,
And briskly went on with his wry reply:
'And let me ask our wise, credulous one,
Whose drum of victory rumbles all alone:
To annul that mortal fiat[73], though right or wrong,

---

[71] ... 'mended fences': see I. 571-592.

[72] In *The Republic*, Plato recalls the Greek poet Pindar as having (in one of his odes) described some celebrant(s) in the Olympic Games as 'plucking the unripe fruits of laughter'. 'Pluck the fruit of victory though unripe' in the line is a modification of the phrase.

Should another be our master's tongue? 280
Perhaps he thinks the cloak of sabotage
Too large to fit the body of a page[74].
The very fiat that prompted us to act
Remains our master's solely to retract;
And what a proxy says to that effect,
One may, yes, accept, or else reject;
And who is smarter than the rest of us
May prove me wrong for all his animus.'
And, again, he ceased to speak (awhile) [75],
And went on speaking with a brooding smile: 290
'Our goal, assured as yet, is find the man
And right his error, as I'm sure we can.
Forgiven he may be; but who is sure?
Not me in the least; and what is more:
It's just our sovereign who can say he is –
With his voice, or else we've heard amiss[76],
Heard amiss from him who claimed our lord
Made him bring to us a different word.'[77]
This was all the leading Faithful said,
Who, having spoken, scratched and shook his head. 300

---

[73] ... 'that mortal fiat': a reference to the monarch's call for the author's head (see. I. 23-24, then I. 31-32).
[74] ... 'a page': the speaker refers to their monarch's page, who brought them the news of the author's absolution.
[75] ... 'ceased to speak (awhile)': paused.
[76] Compare with III. 142.
[77] This intervention by Doom (that is, from III. 271-274 to 277-288, then 291-298), as may be contrasted with the tone and tenor of an earlier intervention by Axe (see III. 66-72, then 75-90), signals a reinforcement of extremism among the Faithfuls. The extremism may be regarded as having taking on a radical hue in the given context.

*   *   *

And the next to speak in Zumba's dream,
Having snatched the vocal reins from him[78],
Was Sword, behind Avenger in their queue;
And, thus, he spoke aloud to all their crew:
'Then we sued for peace[79] on every side;
Now our oneness must be ruined by pride,
The vain, censorious pride of one of us
Whose tactless words have left me at a loss.
It's his pride who ventured to rejoice
And taunt a crewmate with a mocking voice,   310
His pride who hastened to applaud
Himself for having truly understood our lord –
Read him rightly, while the rest of us
Could not link reversion to his curse[80].'
He went on, from having paused his speech:
'And so my backing stays within his reach
Who spoke before me, saying that our lord
Must bring himself to annul his dreaded word.[81]'

*   *   *

And Machete – furious, red and grey –
Snatched the reins from him[82] to have his say: 320
'Yes, the fences mended on our side

---

[78] ... 'him': a reference to Doom, the last speaker.
[79] 'Then we sued for peace....': the speaker alludes to the reconciliation move championed by Doom in I. 571-580 and I. 583-588).
[80] ... 'his curse': a reference to the monarch's call for the author's head, construed as a curse.
[81] '... his dreaded word': (related to 'his curse' – see the preceding footnote).
[82] '... 'him': a reference to Sword, the last speaker.

Have been flattened by some gust of pride;
And I must put support within his reach
Who just dropped our reins of ordered speech.
He's to blame whose tongue, with sooty grime,
Smeared some fruits of joy before their time,
Who stood on shaky grounds to celebrate
A victory – premature – and denigrate
A fellow Faithful with that boast of his,
Which, for sure, was bland and couched amiss.   330
Yes, of the charge we're here to carry out,
To carry out and prove ourselves devout,
It should stay effective, though denounced
By some proxy[83], till by him renounced;
And by 'him' I mean the very voice
To whose words we hardly have a choice,
I mean the lord at whose behest we're here,
Whose command to us was loud and clear:
To find the pen that sketched us with disdain,
And make him lose the chance to write again,   340
Though it means to end his learned life,
To end it in the very heat of strife!'
This, indeed, was all Machete said,
To bring calm to his furious, steaming head.

*   *   *

And Avenger was the next to speak;
His voice, though mild, was very far from weak,
As, numbed, and scratching at his balding head,
He raised his anger-muffled voice and said:
'Must we go in search of why indeed

---

[83] … 'some proxy': a reference to the monarch's page.

We must treat the author as decreed? 350
Let our jester-clown be filled with cheer
And croon the mockery I rejoiced to hear.
Of my ears, I render one to doubt
And turn the other to the horse's mouth,
Though some mulish ear may twitch about
And pay heed to the very page I doubt.'
And he paused, and quickly went ahead,
Speaking, as he gently shook his head:
'Now, I lead that all may follow me
(With he whose folly boasted heartily); 360
But who (to what is past) must stay inclined
May yet ignore my call and stay behind.
By 'what is past' I mean that peace accord
That'd bound our mission with a common cord;
And the cord, severed, and hardly strong,
May still be used to string us all along –
Towards the only goal I'm sure we have:
To make the man's abode an early grave.
The page, the thought of sabotage apart,
I have the choice to listen to my heart; 370
So call it traits of recklessness reborn,
Call it quirky, error, call it scorn,
I go to enforce the order heard at first,
That'd roused in us a burning vengeance-thirst.'
Thus, his grim rejoinder all expressed,
Avenger brought his muffled voice to rest.

*   *   *

Then, to Zumba, would appear a sight:
A being that dazzled for his silvery light;

He had the mien and presence of a god;
In his left hand stood an ivory rod   380
Tipped with gold and bronze and silver hues
Whose constant glimmer you might call diffuse;
His robe was silver-grey, his hair was dark,
A rainbow halo shimmered at his back.
His two feet were the redness of such clay
That, fired, might outshine the light of day
As, before his host, he took a stand,
A sceptre stretching from his other hand;
His golden sandals, firmly tied, were made
From a leather finer far than suede.   390
Having weighed the gloomy ground he broke,
Broke the eerie silence – as he spoke:
'Dear lamb that fears his human sacrifice,
It's Reason – here – before your very eyes;
Your plea to me[84] had reached my distant ears,
And I'd gone to work to fight your fears.
You're not wrong to live in fear of those
Whom I've sent my Stalwarts to oppose;
But stay as right to keep your hopes alive,
For soon the help they bring you shall arrive.'   400
And the radiant guest observed a pause,
And resumed his speech, but changed its course:
'And when their threat is voided as a whole,
And dawn returns to light your clouded soul,
Redeem your fallen mate[85] and love her still,
With such love that reckons not with ill.
Still dare to love her more than tongue can tell,

---

[84] 'Your plea to me': a reference to the author's plea for his (Reason's) intervention (see I. 249-280).
[85] … 'fallen mate': a reference to the author's wife (see footnote number 57).

With a love that'll ever keep her glad and well,
A love that'll shield her from the storms of life,
And make her, most of all, a better wife.'   410
Again, the radiant guest observed a pause,
And went on – with a tone devoid of force:
'Nor ever tend to reckon with the fact,
Nor let it undermine your nuptial pact,
That it was she whom Samson loved at length
That robbed him of his splendour, sight and strength;
But dare to love her more than tongue can tell,
With a love that'll always keep her glad and well,
That'll ever shield her from the storms of life,
And make her, as I said, a better wife;   420
For love is not love if it knows offence
And takes to an endless path of grudges thence.'
And he took a deep breath (stopped awhile),
And went on speaking with a genial smile:
'And this, I say, for what you deem her wrong,
Whence, I sense, your worst dejection sprung:
Such full, unstinting pardon that you crave
Is best for those who, being wronged, forgave.'[86]
Speaking thus, the radiant, godlike guest
Left his sleeping human host at rest.   430

> *   *   *

Now, what followed as hope's silver strand
Fluttered in our author's trembling hand –
As the silver ribbon of his hope
Swayed and wobbled like a jelly rope?
    Now, to him, the Faithfuls reappeared,

---

[86] III. 377-428: Reason visits the author in a dream.

Murmuring, grumbling, muttering – all unheard,
Till, with sudden movements of his head,
The third among their anxious party said
(It was Sword. How bright and double-edged!
Was his stand, his new stand, envisaged   440
As he raised his voice above the pack
To end the grumblings at his front and back?):
'But why permit the scourge of disbelief[87]
To stalk our worthy mission like a thief?
If one of us has wronged us – by default –
To doubt the page for that is double fault.
Perhaps we're able, with some keener sight,
To see how wrong plus wrong amounts to right.
It's strange to hear a proxy lift the spell
That'd willed our target for the flames of hell.   450
Yet, that utter fiends may cease to shout,
Just who deserves no benefit of doubt?
How noble was our strict pedantic school,
Where sane exceptions thrived with every rule?'
And he paused, and went ahead to say
(His eyes adazzle, though his face was grey):
'And hear – a truth I'm happy to affirm:
Now the limber heart in me is firm,
As I hasten to vacate the fence
And boldly take a stand in full defence,   460
In full defence of he whose voice implored,

---

[87] This intervention by Sword (that is, III. 443-454, then 457-466) is indicative of a reinforcement of moderation among the Faithfuls, especially in the light of the news of the absolution of the author by the monarch as conveyed to the Faithfuls by his page. It also contrasts rather sharply with the hard-line positions of Doom (in III. 271-274, 277-288, then 291-298), Machete (in III. 321-342), and Avenger (in III. 349-356, then 359-374).

Implored our crew to rethink with our lord
The vengeful threat that hangs over the man,
And forgive him as, yes, we truly can.
The man is pardoned, and he told us why:
Sometimes to sin is not to have to die.'[88]
And he paused and gently scratched his head,
Rubbed his eyes, and calmly went ahead:
'Then, to come apart and speak the truth,
Against the terror of some fierce untruth: 470
It's worse than godless that a faith should kill
To avenge itself against some wrong or ill.'

*   *   *

Then to Zumba would appear a lad[89]
Whose translucent mien was far from glad,
As, leaping, stag-like, he approached the place
Where royal Reason shed his rays of grace;
I mean the plateau at whose verdant feet
You'd hear the pigeons coo, the young sheep bleat;
Where shepherd-nature, with her rod of haze,
Drove her feral flocks to drink and graze.   480
The plains stretched farther than the eye could go;
There crystal brooks remained in constant flow,
Watering slopes and valleys through the year,
Raising food for rodents and for deer.
The glistening greenness of that sea of grass
In the gloaming glowed like burnished brass,
And by noon the sun's prismatic beams

---

[88] The line echoes I. 508 and III. 144.
[89] ... 'a lad': a reference to the page Reason sent to recall the Stalwarts (see
II. 409-418).

Left tints of silver on the grass and streams.
Only dawn might leave that meadow green –
A shade of green few eyes have ever seen;   490
A shade that, set against a fountain-stream,
Dazzled even in our author's dream;
A shade of green – a rare, mysterious kind –
That proved a dreamer needn't be colour-blind.
    The crags were stepping stones towards the top
Where Reason sipped from mild reflection's cup,
Where pensive Reason, seated on his throne,
Sipped his meditations – all alone,
Where he sat alone, in Zumba's dream,
And, ringed with quiet, waited for his team –   500
Waited for the Stalwarts – one and all –
Whom he'd sent the said lad to recall.
    And Reason, startled by the lad in sight,
Panned his royal view from left to right;
And, steadying now his gaze, inquired at first:
'Why return to me without the rest?'
And the lad would stutter in reply,
Having half-restrained a nagging sigh:
'They're cau-cau- caught on earth
By faith's vexatious wrath;   510
They've be-be- been seized by those
You sent them to oppose.'
    And Reason, doubly curious and alert,
Wondered how his hopes could come to that;
For, yes, the news of that occasion stung,
And proved his joyous expectations wrong.
(How the future lies beyond the ken
Of all-discerning Reason, as of men!
Even God – in ruing his making man –

Confessed that man's perversion beat his plan;[90]   520
The said regret – were it plausible –
Would also prove God's vision fallible,
And locate Reason, God, humanity,[91]
Beneath the spectre of uncertainty,
And situate faith beneath the self-same shade,
Where the unknown is lord, the royal head.
But can the omniscient One, indeed,
Have been thus inclined to rue his deed?
Can that professed all-knowing that is God,
Be inclined to give his said regret a nod?)   530

         *   *   *

    Did not Reason, in his next request,
Ask his eye from earth to 'tell the rest',
Thinking that the lad had seen it all
And had some long proceedings to recall
Of how the Faithfuls swooped down on his five
Before that crucial moment would arrive,
That moment he had programmed to forestall
Their harm in battle through their planned recall?
    And didn't the courier-lad attempt his best
To answer fully to his lord's request   540
But found his memory terror-dulled, and strained,

---

[90] The couplet, i.e. III. 519-520 (with the subsequent three) explores the possible implications of the declaration: 'And the LORD was sorry that He had made man on the earth, and He was grieved in His heart.' (Genesis 6: 6, NKJV). As the next couplet (III. 521-522) suggests, this declaration should be examined in the light of the contrary assertion that 'God *is* not man...,/Nor a son of man, that He should repent ...' (Numbers 23:19, NKJV).

[91] ... 'humanity': humankind.

As he'd found his power of speech constrained –
When he stammered in his last reply,
Having half-restrained a nagging sigh?[92]
And this, I recall, was the much he said,
That lodged more worries in his master's head:
'I went down, as prompted, to the earth,
Traced our Stalwarts through its length and breadth,
And, just before I'd lose hope, they appeared;
But your newer stand was undeclared,   550
Nor could I make to pronounce their recall,
Before a group of three would seize us all,
And take us prisoner by the force of arms,
Rattling – as they were – with sundry charms[93].
Yet, they keep with them our stalwart five –
Ringed with terror, numbed and half-alive.
Our captors seek a ransom for the five,
A ransom if they must be freed alive;
"The ransom must be Zumba," they have said,
Who seized us in a battle undeclared,   560
And set me free to "run" and tell you this:
"The man must come to face his nemesis!"'
        And so what Burns[94] has said of men and mice,
And the well-laid schemes they oft device,
May apply to godlike beings who plan with care
To make worse or mend our earthly sphere.
        And Reason cast a long look at the ground

---

[92] The line echoes III. 508.
[93] ... 'sundry charms': see I. 40.
[94] The couplet (i.e. III. 563-564) alludes to the observation by the Scottish poet Robert Burns (in his ballad titled 'To A Mouse') that 'The best laid schemes o' mice an' men/Gang aft agley,/An' lea'e us nought but grief an' pain,/For promis'd joy!'

And raised his sight, and swung it round and round;
And, again, he coolly sought to know
(Having wiped the sweat across his brow):   570
'What reduced their band from five to three?
The cause of such decline is hard to see.'
To that the courier-lad could not reply,
And so he simply let the question lie[95];
For the split occurred behind his view,
So distant as to leave him not a clue.
It came behind the heels of that discord
On which the Faithfuls argued on the word
That sought to douse their passion for revenge
And instil in them a gracious change,   580
A change of mind towards the man they sought
To bring his labours and his life to naught;
For while the heedless three inflamed with rage,
And frothed in their anger, their umbrage,
The third and fifth embraced the later word,
And returned, with its source[96], to meet their lord.
'They're blessed that hear and yield,' the fifth had said,
As he urged his faction to renounce the raid
(The vengeance-raid to take the author's life,
A venture that might plunge them into strife),   590
While the others went on with their quest:
'To quench the author at our lord's behest.'
(Thus, Sword and Axe became the absent two:
Not among the hostage-taking crew,
And the third was him their monarch sent
To urge their five-strong party to relent;
Whose mission, thanks to misoneism,

---

[95] ... 'lie': rest.
[96] ... 'its source': a reference to the monarch's page.

Had now spawned a sort of schism).

      *   *   *

    Then, as though his knowing was rewound,
Reason let his royal voice resound,   600
Speaking brusquely of their band whose lord
Had sent for baying for the author's blood:
'Their souls in monocle, indeed half-blind,
They go to ruin an author and his mind,
Stumbling down the bouldery path of faith,
To hear our sober side they could not wait?'

    And Reason, mounted on a higher ground,
Waited, as his anxious thoughts unwound,
And while he waited muttered to himself
(As he focused on a granite shelf):   610
'I still think that strife cannot be proper;
No weapon fashioned for my use shall prosper[97];
I'll go, unhurried, with the one they seek,
Though his hope may now be worse than bleak;
If the power of thought cannot avail,
Then the force of strife must not prevail;
If persuasion cannot help our cause,
Nor, I think, can any lethal force.
To explore the argument of grace – I go,
And take my thoughts for arrows and for bow!'   620
    Thus, sweet Reason turned his back on strife
And yet was keen to save our author's life.

---

[97] The pronouncement – the entire line – is rather antithetical to 'No weapon formed against you shall prosper.' (Isaiah 54:17, NKJV).

Canto IV

*Reason, in the company of his
page, descends to the earth, and
returns to the author (whom he
had visited in a dream, which
persists) and persuades him to
accompany them to the monarch's
court where, having listened to
his intercessional plea, the
monarch affirms his reprieve for
the author, and other related
occurrences.*

Poetry, wear your charms, lead the troops of letters
To seek bound souls and break their iron fetters.

*   *   *

Solemn seeker who must go before[98]
Take me yet in tow and tell me more,
Lest the prospects tire my wandering eyes
As alps on conquered alps on alps arise.[99]
Set pen to the parchment of my soul;
Lead on, as I strain to reach the goal,
The goal you've set to calm the nerves of earth
And save an author from a prowling death;   10

---

[98] See III. 183 and the associated footnote.
[99] Lest... arise: an adaptation of Alexander Pope's 'Soon the prospects tire our wandering eyes/As hills peep over hills, and alps on alps arise' (from *Essay on Criticism*).

The goal to explore a posture deemed perverse
And end a conflict in the bounds of verse.[100]
Mine's to yield, yours the faith and skill,
A pliant tool to fashion out your will;
And yet it's yours to plead the cause of life,
Yours to sow our peace amid their strife,
Yours to change an anguished author's fate,
Yours to censure rancour, war and hate.

*   *   *

And Reason went, descending to the earth,
Descending to the earth with bated breath,   20
As – having tried to free his heart from fear –
His page (and courier) followed at his rear.
His grizzled hair and beard, his brawny frame,
His muscles rippling to his heart's acclaim,
His dour demeanour and his furrowed face,
Were veils to hide a placid mien of grace;
And how like the herd who, now severe, now mild,
Led the Flock of Israel through the wild[101],
Though no tablets waited in his hand
For smashing on some idolatrous band,   30
As, yes, he went, descending to the earth,
Descending to the earth with bated breath,
Climbing down the plateau of a realm
Where he holds the reins and keeps the helm.
And didn't the thought engage his quiet mind,
Of a trend he'd always deemed 'unkind'?
That some use saccharined tipple

---

[100] Compare IV. 11-12 with I. 9-10.
[101] Wild: wilderness.

To keep their hold on people;
That faith remains the tipple mostly used:
'A strong-sweet wine, like opium when abused.'   40
The thought or, yes, reflection, came behind
A musing that had quite engaged his mind:
'The hand that steals today may heal tomorrow,
And pass to doing good from causing sorrow;
So should a God of mercy lop it off
And not, for mercy, try to show it love?
Thus, the tongue now steeped in heresy
May, given time, profess orthodoxy.'
And the musing also came behind
Another that'd as well engaged his mind: 50
'The faithful should leave God to fight his fight;
They shouldn't fight for him and deem it right;
For God, granted omni-potency,
Should need no help to prove his potency.
Or is it right to deem it right to fight
For such a being we deem supreme in might?'

                    *   *   *

   And now, with worries trickling down his mind,
The pensive sovereign asked the one behind[102]:
'Did you bring a sprig of peace with you,
A branch of olive fresh and wet with dew?'   60
Whereupon the lad brandished the sprig,
Whose glint, he'd thought, would startle and intrigue,
Though high up in their tableland abode,
An olive sprig could grow from any node.

---

[102] The one behind (likewise 'the good lad' in IV. 72): a reference to
Reason's page.

(Some 'Mountain Olive' was their 'Tree of State',
Potent, as they thought, to ward off hate;
A cambric pennant was their 'Flag of State',
Potent, as they thought, to repel hate;
A blonde-white pigeon was their 'Bird of State',
Potent, as they thought, to dispel hate.)   70

      *   *   *

And now the pensive sovereign flushed with pride
As he gently drew the good lad to his side;
And – step by step – the two would spend the day
Climbing down a steep and rocky way,
A bouldery way that led from butte to butte,
And often through some sheer and slippery route.
And more-than-midway from some rocky peak,
The younger one behind began to speak;
And these, I recall, were the things he said,
As he gently shook and scratched his head: 80
'Such faith,' you'd tell us, 'may be viewed as ill
That takes away the bridle from our zeal,
And then imparts its dogmas to our minds, without
The scope to mix belief with doubt.
And you've had occasion to propound
That a faith unquestioned stays unfound;
And such faith, you'd add, cannot be deemed
To have had its moral soul redeemed.'
And he paused, and pondered for a while,
And licked his lips, and went on with a smile: 90
'You have further said, and dared disproof,
That a faith must hinge its claims on proof;
And then you would say – and I agree –

That substance is the surest proof we see;
That when no substance can secure belief,
May logic come to ward off disbelief.
But, far from such views, permit me to ask
(And maybe put your trusted mind to task):
May our school of thought be well-deplored
For deeming God-pervaded nature God?   100
Our minds are linked with many a feckless wing
For seeing God as lodged in everything;
For thus, our critics say, they cannot fly
To meet God in his rightful place on high.
They'd urge that all diffusion weakens strength,
And ours is sure to offend God at length;
Our minds, they'd add, diffuse Divinity
Both as Godhead and the Trinity,
And renders weaker, till infinity,
God's very essence, which is unity.   110
So may our school of thought be well-deplored
For deeming God-pervaded nature God?'

        *   *   *

And sovereign Reason, whom the lad addressed,
Listened till his voice would come to rest,
Whereupon he coughed to clear his throat,
And gave this answer – on a candid note:
'You're best advised to view our school of thought
As linking thought with either flux or naught.
It's still the timeless rubric of that school
That thought should never be a stagnant pool.'   120
And he coughed to clear his throat again,
And then resumed his speech with lesser strain:

'Now look down to the earth – espy the Nile,
Fix a gaze upon its stream awhile;
You see: its liquid substance stays the same,
And restless currents do not change its name,
Nor does ceaseless motion change its course.
Now freeze the fluid impressions in a pause.
Then towards the Dead Sea shift your view
And glean impressions from its stagnant clue –   130
Of how stagnation bodes decay and death
For thought and all the mind can bring to birth,
And how change is the harbinger of all
We give the name of progress, great or small;
And by change I mean the very form
Of change that alters but does not deform,
Like the change you saw along the Nile,
A steady stream through many a thousand mile.'
And here the speaker, Reason, coughed again,
And then resumed with even lesser strain: 140
'Then, to your question, let it just suffice
To say (with no intention to surprise)
That nature, I have come to think of late,
Is best perceived as man's subordinate.
I contradict myself? O well, yes;
Progress, to my mind, entails no less.'
And he coughed again, and shook his head,
And gathered up his thoughts, and went ahead:
'I should like to explore to what effect
Those views on nature must admit defect   150
And so deserve discarding as I have,
And burial in some philosophic grave;
But thought, for now, were better put to use
To right the error of our friend's abuse;

Rather, let's by means of thought undo
The very wrong that now detains our crew
And win reprieve for he who sought our face
And thwart his ruin that'll mean our sure disgrace;
So let nature be the world she is,
To dwell on her will steer our task amiss,   160
Though I deem it worthy to be stressed:
My views on her have altered, and progressed;
For though still awed by her divinity,
She's less the Deity she was once to me.'
And Reason coughed again, and shook his head,
And rubbed his blurry eyes, and went ahead:
'Just how do abstract views of God avail
Our friend, the author, in his long travail?
And how do they avail the world of men
That swarms with many a bigots-ridden den?'   170
And he coughed again, and scratched his head,
And cleared his stuffy nose, and went ahead:
'But let me just proceed to say, or ask,
The while we hasten to our pressing task:
Can that being be God – "the Ultimate" –
Who by mere default controls our fate,
Or who – without the reins from you and me –
May fill our world with woe and misery?
What God is, who "he" is and where "he" is,
Our minds may ever strive to grasp but miss!   180
(The earth is sphere-like, though it had been 'flat';
So let faith object and err at that).
What's God with earthquakes and with hurricanes,
The tortured anguish of life's ceaseless pains?'

*   *   *

And Reason dammed his stream of words (awhile),
And (then) released it with a genial smile
(Yes, he dammed the fluid words on his tongue
And, smiling broadly, let it roll along):
'Yet I think it's worth my while to add
(For truth must even out, my gentle lad)   190
That faith, revealed, may raise our certainty
To grasp the truth of true divinity;
But how "true" or "sure" the certainty
May have more to do with mere belief
Than if the very faith we choose to hold
Is truly worth its measured weight in gold;
That is, if it's known ancestral line
Is such that links us to some true divine[103];
But such a rare link can we claim for sure
And not appear presumptuous to the core?   200
Or should any faith so claim, perchance,
And not deserve the charge of arrogance?'
And Reason, having made a gentle pause,
Steered his speech towards another course:
'Now let's rather with our thought contrive
To save our protégé[104] and stalwart five.
That's the task for which we approach the earth,
Such use of thought more truly proves its worth.
With such a grim challenge before our eyes,
Why bask in thought – an abstract exercise?'   210
And Reason paused his speech, he paused again,
And then proceeded – calmly – to explain:
'We can guide the eyes of faith to see

---

[103] Divine: divinity.
[104] Our protégé: a reference to the author (see also II. 198).

How faith inclines to gain by heresy;
Or didn't Buddha, Jesus, Mohammed,
By voicing dissent, move some faith ahead?
The wish is wrong, and doubly wrong the strife,
That faith should lead an unexamined life;
And when she's piqued by censure, I would wish
She learns to hold her fury by the leash;   220
A critic's flak may yet improve our light,
Though his tone were judged as impolite;
And some views we'd rather curb by force
May involve some moral posture deemed perverse,[105]
Like those courageous Luther[106] voiced, of old,
Which, deemed heretic in their novel mould,
Would yet direct a straying age aright,
And rectify a faith's distorted light.
Who wants a ship of faith to meet her wreck,
Whose truth, told promptly, jolts her crew awake?   230
And this call for Zumba's head, I think, is odd,
For it pretends to the judgment seat of God.
Do not judge,[107] the Christ-divine had urged,
For all was found deficient who was judged.'
Here he dammed again his vocal stream
As they[108] faded out of Zumba's dream.

* * *

Now, in Zumba's dream, the five[109] appeared,

---

[105] Compare with I. 9.
[106] Martin Luther (1483-1546): German theologian and leader, in Germany, of the Protestant Reformation.
[107] See Luke 6:7 (NIV).
[108] They: a reference to Reason and his page.

And their groaning monotones were heard:
The tortured moaning of the very five
Who, indeed, were captured all alive;   240
Captured and detained as hostages
'To be used as meat for sausages';
For that – a mocking threat? – was what they said
Who seized the five in that rebellious raid,
And then dispatched the lad to make request
For a ransom in return for all the rest.
'The ransom must be Zumba,' he'd relayed,
From those who won 'a battle undeclared'.[110]

       *   *   *

And Doom, now posing as the captor's guide,
Used a stick to poke a captive's side,   250
As he muttered, just beneath his breath:
'This can pierce his lungs with sudden death,
Tied up, as he is, to stagnancy,
And lost, as all his mates, to clemency,
Unless our monarch can himself be here
To speak up for their pardon to my ear;
Else, they'll sink in misery to their ears;
More grief than known to grieving shall be theirs,
Guests to us, as cheerful and as free
As bound with thongs to immobility,   260
As glad as tortured by this able hand
That's proud to put to shame their heathen band,
That's propped the ruthless ritual to distort
The psyche of each captive and his thought.

---

[109] The five: a reference to the Stalwarts.
[110] Compare IV. 247-248 with III. 559-560.

I pledge to God to toil by slow degrees
To put each pagan captive through disease.'
And glancing at his mates on either side,
The speaker thundered forth with martial pride:
'We may have to take our quarry home
And simply let the sought-for ransom roam,   270
Take them home for roasting at the stake
Meant for him whose life we wish to take.
Nor should we reckon with their blameless state;
Isn't a hostage just some pawn of fate?'
    He coughed, hemmed, shook his head,
And smiling with some hesitation said:
'There's no greater boon from heaven above
Than loving what you do or doing what you love.
And – yes! – I love to show the infidel
That their unbelief must burn in hell.'   280
    Here another speaker took the cue
(Another member of their rebel crew):
'What to do with these we now detain?
To keep them, as they are, in serious pain,
To keep them ever less and less alive,
Till our favoured ransom shall arrive;
And if we can't compel him to emerge,
Then five birds can make for one at large.'
    And then another speaker took the cue:
The very last among their rebel crew;   290
And here's my record of the things he said,
Spoken, as he gently shook his head:
'Fate should rather bring our sole request
Than lose these victims at our lord's behest.'
And the speaker paused, and went ahead,
Speaking, as he gently scratched his head:

'And this waiting, with these lives at stake:
Numbed with terror for his haughty sake,
For his haughty sake whose very guilt
Was to smear our faith with written filth!   300
But then I'll urge restraint on all of us,
Hell-bent, as we are, to enforce the curse
That our master placed upon his head,
For which we hold these captives in his stead.'
And the speaker paused, and cleared his throat,
And went on speaking on a cautious note:
'Won't our master charge us with disdain,
That we made his courier speak in vain,
Though the tacky state we seemed to face
Was either spurn his word or take disgrace?   310
Yet, we might stem his wrath's severity
If we blamed it on the lad's obscurity
And told our master: "If his words were clear,
What could be our reason not to hear,
And having heard comply with what we heard,
And pulled back from our mission undeterred?"
And the deterrence, explained by me,
Will be ascribed to that obscurity.
Thus we'll douse the fury of his blame,
And go to keep his favour all the same.'   320
And he paused, and gently scratched his back,
And went on speaking, having changed his tack:
'Of what to do with him, for whom we wait,
For whom we hold these hostages as bait,
Let our leader tell our threesome crew,
While we have the five to keep in view.'

*   *   *

And Doom, their leader, was the next to speak,
With a voice you'd deem unduly weak:
'We just must try to satisfy the lord
That rules perdition with an iron sword;[111]   330
And it's all to him the ransom goes,
His choice to spend or save it, I suppose;
Hence I pledge to take it down to him, down
To him who wears our iron crown,
That he may truly exercise his right
To pardon, as we've learnt, the author's slight.'
Speaking thus, that leader of their crew,
With his rebels, passed from Zumba's view.
(The dreaming author, having heard them speak,
Felt his worries inching to their peak).   340

*   *   *

Now the author saw the other lad[112]
Looking limp and very far from glad;
He saw him looking limp before a throne
Where, of course, the monarch sat alone.
On his left and right were Sword and Axe,
Looking drained and eager to relax.
And now the anxious pair of returnees,
Bent to scratch an itch across their knees,
Before they'd genuflect – to greet the one
Seated firmly on their iron throne;   350
And he gave his page a sign to speak;
Zumba heard him speak; he sounded weak:

---

[111] Compare with I. 92.
[112] The other lad: a reference to the monarch's page.

'I met the five on earth and told them all
That you'd sent me for their full recall;
Sword and Axe agreed to come with me;
The rest did not return, as you can see;
They'd rather go ahead, it seems to me,
And hunt their quarry[113] with tenacity,
Go ahead with more than doubled zeal
To make his "demolition" more than real.'   360

    And the monarch shook his head and sighed,
Shook his head and sighed, and then replied:
'You made my message clear, so very clear,
Which was why the two with you could hear,
And hearing give full assent to my voice;
The other three did not obey by choice
And shall have to share the noxious blame
That their choice may bring, the foul acclaim.'
And he paused, a lengthy pause it was,
And then resumed his speech, but changed its course: 370
'Now, of their "quarry", I must bring to light:
His head is not the bone for which I fight[114];
It's that unflattering liberty of thought:
To curb its influence I had ever sought;
And poised to see its end, my envious eyes
Had seen him as a fitting sacrifice,
Or, better put, a threat which, brought to naught,
Will help to curb the spread of liberal thought;
But now, in retrospect, I feel depressed
To link myself with such a shameful quest: 380
To make his "demolition" more than real[115]

---

[113] Their quarry: a reference to the author.
[114] The bone...fight: the bone of contention.

And thereby undermine a great ideal,
The unfettered-thought ideal he represents,
Whose sure and steady spread our faith resents.'
And the monarch paused, and flashed a smile,
As if to say: 'I've purged my heart of bile,'
And (done with smiling) went on with his speech,
With the threesome[116] at his vocal reach:
'I'm inclined to pardon him, of course;
I do so as a gesture of remorse;   390
Truly, I have pardoned him, indeed,
And must urge on you a self-same deed;
Inclined, I also am, to quash that curse;
Tell the others when they're back to us
(Nor should we waste upon the stake or cross
A mind that's shown his kind of stark remorse);
I've quashed the curse, the curse I'd placed on him.'
    And the author heard him in his dream.
He heard him till they faded out of sight,
As the twilight dims – before the night –   400
To make way for that whiteness of palm wine
With which a jolly moon is wont to shine.

*   *   *

And now, at Zumba's side, their king appeared,
Their king who lost 'a battle undeclared'[117];
With him was his bold, disciplic lad;[118]

---

[115] Compare with IV. 360.
[116] The threesome: a contextual reference to Sword, Axe and the monarch's page.
[117] Compare with III. 560 and IV. 248.
[118] Bold, disciplic lad: a reference to Reason's page.

Their robes were loose; their feet were sandal-clad;
And both guests stood erect beside his couch,
Where his cat was resting in a crouch;
The cat, more black than pitch, a Bombay cat,
Rested on a blue-and-greenish mat, 410
A carpet plush and hairy like its coat,
A mat adorned with many a sailing boat;
A fine gondola and a yacht were there,
And a canoe – floating in the air!
And a houseboat sailed beside a skiff
Near a setting like a coral reef.
And need I make a mention of the sloop
And the raft that led the seaward troupe
On those broad companionable streams
Flowing down that rug of Zumba's dreams? 420
    And soon the trickles of a story ran
From the sovereign to the dreaming man:
From its fountain when the former heard
The plea for urgent help the latter made,
It trickled down a wet and winding route,
Gathering fluid momentum with its truth,
Down to when the former sent his five
To make sure that the latter stays alive;
And then to how 'this very lad[119] was sent' –
To recall the five – and how he went; 430
And to how some ransom must be sent,
Or some lives in danger will be spent,
'Lives held hostage with some iron sword
Sharpened by some godly overlord;
Their innocence,' he'd add, 'would go to waste,
Unless we sent the ransom, and with haste;

---

[119] This very lad: a contextual reference to Reason's page.

Arise and let us go, without delay,
Our gentle pleas may coax their wrath away.'
    Here, the author stretched a lengthy sigh,
And gently cut in with a faint reply: 440
'If, at length, their wrath proves adamant,
Who becomes the ransom they must want?'
Whereupon the sovereign one replied,
Nibbling at the truth he would not hide:
'Now, we have to reason for the best,
And reason for the best by trusting first.
No night, though more dark than yours and mine,
Can quite defy the light of faith to shine;
The Providential, should the need arise,
Shall send some ransom for our sacrifice.   450
Or don't we reckon it a pride with him
To hold all human life in great esteem?
Indeed, should the unlikely need arise,
He'll spring on us a ransom of surprise.'
    Here, though still asleep, the man arose,
And, having risen, struck a willing pose.
They stepped into the brilliance of a night
Awash with moonbeams and with stellar light:
The hosts of heaven, in a grand parade,
Were dressed in starry garments, overhead;   460
And soon – how soon! – the mortal follower,
Walked into a noxious atmosphere,
And drew a whiff of such ominous breath
As when a victim smells impending death:
He thought himself the ransom, and was numb,
But yet adjudged it proper to succumb.
Yes, he felt like one that bore within
The knife and faggot for his offering,

As his every step approached the place
Where death, he thought, would quickly close his case,   470
And, taking him, return the lives at stake,
Seized and taken hostage for his sake.

*   *   *

And further in his slumber Zumba saw
Himself before the monarch's 'Throne of Law'.
Safe-in-scabbard stood his sundry swords;
The hostage takers cringed beneath his words,
The captives, now unbound and standing free,
With Zumba, heard their lord advance his plea;
The monarch, with a cocked, attentive head,
Listened hard and well as Reason said: 480
'Shouldn't faith as yet embrace such men
Who fall from good and rise to good again?
Or can a faith that wastes them in disgrace
Retain its rightful claim to godly grace?
There is more a noble faith can do than
Shut the door of grace on any man.
Show, then, the truly pious step to take,
As the man[120] is fastened to the stake:
To douse flambeaux of passion, and forgive,
And thereby grant our friend your full reprieve   490
Or move to enact his everlasting fall,
And thereby mock the grace that pardons all.
Perhaps we're both on course to losing face
Should our hearts ignore this pull of grace
And its bounties whence we've ever drawn,
And which, being God's, cannot be overdrawn.

---

[120] The man (likewise 'our friend' in IV. 484): a reference to the author.

And shouldn't we all be channels whence its reach
Should extend to every sinful breach?'
He felt the tension rise from low to high,
And stopped to hear his royal host's reply.   500
  And the monarch, fully in control,
Would let the answer on his tongue unroll;
He'd prime his voice, and then proceed to tell
How, 'enraged', he'd 'willed the man to hell',
And how, 'with due dispatch', his crew[121] 'was sent
To ensure it's where his afterlife was spent';
And to how, 'divested of such rage',
He'd later send his 'nimble courier-page'
To 'call back' to his realm 'the earthbound crew.
That,' he went on, was 'the overview;   510
For much, and very much, transpired withal;
I'll save your time by not recounting all.'
And having paused, and waited for a while,
He went on, speaking, with a genial smile:
'Now, at last, I'm glad the man is here
To hear my new, congenial voice declare:
He is reprieved, pardoned, absolved, forgiven,
And all my grace you seek for him is given.
Our peace shall hence enfold him, as before.
He should go and try to sin no more[122].   520
The face of piety is a changing face,
And thus can turn its look from wrath to grace.'
  And he looked towards his loyalists
And, pointing at the author, told them this:

---

[121] His crew: a reference to the Faithfuls.
[122] The line attempts to synthesise the statements: '...Sin no more, lest a worse thing come upon you' (John 5:14, NKJV) and '...Neither do I condemn you; go and sin no more' (John 8:11, NKJV).

'Here, again, the salt regains its savour,[123]
The penitent returning to our favour;
Feel free to shake his hand in hate-release
And put flesh on this skeleton of peace.'
    The sound of silence boomed from wall to wall,
With the monarch having said his all;   530

And Reason, having crossed his chest, replied
(With the author standing by his side):
'I give this olive branch on his behalf,
With this white ensign, its other half.'

                *   *   *

    And Zumba woke up from his dreamful sleep
And felt a rare relief as sharp as deep.

                *   *   *

    And you, whose sole delight is verse or truth,
Whose ways I learnt, untutored, as a youth,
To you let come the glory for our toil,
While the seas beneath the sun may boil,   540
Having dared to plead the cause of sense,
And win full pardon for our friend's offence.
It's of you I speak, my Muse, of you,
Ever calm as night and soft as dew,
You who gave my heart its vocal cords,
And tuned my ears to the music of words;
Humble was my task, humbly I depart,
And leave you with a warm and grateful heart.

---

[123] See Luke 14:34, NKJV.

APPENDIX
(Music Scores)

The Roaring Rage

From *The Heresad* (Canto I, lines 13-32)

Music by **Ikeogu Oke**
Arr. by **Adeogun Adebowale**

Music Typesetting by **Jude Nwankwo**

2   The Roaring Rage

bring   be - fore   my throne   his   up - right   head!   Ig -

nore his soul or what may prove its   luck: Rath-er   lose a   lamb than for-go all the

flock: For   such   a   man,   if   left   to thrive   on   earth,   May

void our ho-nour and en-force our   death.   Yes,   death's the pro-per fate that a-waits

him.   I   charge   you   now   to move and   quench   his   dream.   Un-

gra - cious though   I   know   this   is,   let   Zum - ba   die!   I've

marked   a   val - ley   where   his   corpse   will   lie."_____

The Forlorn Supplication

From *The Heresad* (Canto II, lines 247-276)

Music by **Ikeogu Oke**
Arr. *by* **Adeogun Adebowale**

Music Typesetting by **Jude Nwankwo**

The Forlorn Supplication

named your bea-con for my fel-low men.   Come down quick-ly lest I come to

rue   That   I chose to   pitch   my tent   with   you,

As I've large-ly rued my faith in   men,   Whose   ways with me, for now, sug-gest dis-

dain."   And our au - thor   (ra - ther tongue - in - cheek)   Ob-

served a pause, and then re-sumed to   speak: "Yet, in my dis-tress, I have come to

know   A   thing   or two   for which   my tact   may   grow;   That

one   man's pain   is a-no - ther man's   glo - ry,   And

one man's grief a-no-ther's sweet sto - ry."   And our au-thor, Zum-ba, paused a-

gain,   And   went   a - head   to plead,   and plead   with   pain:

Please se-cure my falter-ing hu-man   trust,   And   save the i-ron of my faith from

rust.   Move   to void   the price placed on   my   head;

Save   your friend   from   this   un - nerv - ing   dread."

The Bold Resolution

From *The Heresad* (Canto III, lines 607-620)

Music *by* **Ikeogu Oke**
Arr. *by* **Adeogun Adebowale**

ad lib.

Music Typesetting by **Jude Nwankwo**

The Great Submission

From *The Heresiad* (Canto IV, lines 455-472)

Music by **Ikeogu Oke**
Arr. by **Adeogun Adebowale**

Music Typesetting by **Jude Nwankwo**

2   The Great Submission

cumb.   Yes,   he felt   like one   that bore   with - in   The

knife and fag-got   for his of - fer - ing,   As his eve - ry step ap-proached the

place   Where death, he thought, would quick-ly close his case,   And,

tak-ing him, re-turn the lives at   stake,   Seized and ta-ken hos - tage for his

sake

Printed in the United States
By Bookmasters